WRITING UNCOVERED PUT AND CALL COMBINATIONS

Earn Two Option Premiums
from One Margin Requirement
on Individual Stocks and
Exchange Traded Funds (ETFs)
Without Owning Them

Paul D. Kadavy

Arrow Publications

✳ ARROW PUBLICATIONS
P.O. Box 19464
Fountain Hills, Arizona 85269-9464
E-Mail: arrowpublications@cox.net
Web site: www.arrowpublications.net

Manufactured in the United States of America
ISBN 0-9715514-6-4
Library of Congress Control Number: 2004093435

WRITING UNCOVERED PUT AND CALL COMBINATIONS

QUESTIONS FOR THE AUTHOR

Mr. Kadavy maintains a question and answer section on the Arrow Publications Web site. Readers who would like to ask him a question regarding one of his books or about implementation of the strategies contained within them can go to the Web page and review the questions and answers that have been previously posted. If the question is new, the reader should click on the "E-mail Me" button and submit the question. A personal response will be provided. If the question would be of broader use to the reading audience, Mr. Kadavy's response will be posted on the Web site. These questions and answers can be a valuable tool for additional learning.

For questions, go to:

www.arrowpublications.net/Questions.html

CONTENTS

PREFACE

Writing "uncovered" (also sometimes referred to as "naked") put and call option "combinations" (the simultaneous writing, or sale, of put and call options where shares are not owned by the investor at the time of the transaction) can present a very attractive opportunity for option investors in taxable accounts (uncovered writing is generally not offered for retirement accounts). For the option investor, the simultaneous writing of a put and a call on the same security can provide, as we will see, a two-fold steady stream of income utilizing the same margin requirement if structured properly. It can also provide a chance to purchase shares of stock at a lower than current market price, if that is an investor's objective. This book will give you the theoretical and practical tools necessary to develop and implement an investment strategy that will provide the opportunity to achieve significant investment returns through writing uncovered put and call combinations on individual stocks and Exchange Traded Funds (ETFs).

This book is for investors who are proficient in covered call writing (shares are owned to back the option transaction) and who have preferably also engaged in uncovered put writing (where shares are not owned, but the transaction is supported by a margin requirement). With exposure to these investment disciplines an investor would be in a position to determine whether his or her knowledge, experience and appetite for risk is sufficient to consider taking the leap into writing uncovered combinations.

This is a big leap. Combination option writing is not by any means new, but it is new to almost all individual investors. While it offers the opportunity to significantly increase investment returns, it clearly also increases risk of loss, even if the option writer takes the disciplined approach described in this book.

Unlike covered call writing and put writing (if utilized under similar risk/reward characteristics as covered call writing), an uncovered combination writer may need to stay in frequent or under some circumstances constant touch with the market. As a combination writer, you would likely not want to take a trip for several days unless you were able to check in with your broker, either by computer or on the phone. And, depending on how your uncovered short positions are doing, there are even times when you would not be comfortable being away from the market long enough to play a round of golf! This is not because you are necessarily doing frequent trading. It is because of the need for quick action to close out a position to mitigate losses if it moves against you beyond your pre-defined parameters.

Writing uncovered combinations is probably not a manageable investment strategy for an investor who has a full-time job that would preclude the ability to check on the market from time to time. And in circumstances where action is necessary, you must have the ability to drop everything and devote your full attention to your option positions.

For investors who have time to watch the market, who have the comfort that comes from knowledge and experience with other option writing strategies, and fully understand and are prepared to take additional risk, writing uncovered option combinations offers the opportunity for very high returns at a time when the overall long-term outlook for investment returns, both equity and fixed income, seems to be at very low tide.

We have always been taught that if an investment opportunity offers greater returns, it must correspondingly carry with it greater risks. That is most certainly true of the investment opportunity on which this book is based. For that reason, much attention will be devoted to detailing the risks that are involved so that you, the reader, can make an informed decision whether this strategy is in alignment with your willingness to assume greater risk. The book offers a program with numerous opportunities to mitigate that risk. A discussion of technical analysis also offers tools that can help control risk and enhance investment returns. If you make an informed decision to proceed and use a consistent plan to limit risk, the opportunities for very sizeable investment returns abound.

* * * * *

The reader should be aware that brokerage commissions and other transaction costs have not been included in the investment calculations for the examples used in order to simplify the subject matter presented. Such costs are discussed in this book and would need to be considered in actual calculations. Provisions have been made to customize the software available with this book to fit the commission schedule of the user's brokerage firm.

Prior to trading any option, an investor must receive a copy of *Characteristics and Risks of Standardized Options*. A copy may be obtained from the investor's broker or on the Internet at www.cboe.com.

Paul D. Kadavy

NOTE REGARDING THE MICROSOFT EXCEL® TEMPLATES DISCUSSED IN THIS BOOK

We have created three custom Excel® file templates that will facilitate your use of the program outlined in this book.

The use of these templates will greatly assist you with the calculations necessary to make quality decisions using the combination option writing program. Now, or when you are ready to use these Excel® files, please send an e-mail to arrowpublications@cox.net requesting the "combinations files." We will promptly provide you with the files by return e-mail. Your e-mail address will *never* be sold or given to anyone.

If you do not have a computer, many libraries offer computers for use at no charge and they often have Excel® software installed on them which will enable you to run the above-mentioned templates.

If you have a computer but do not have Microsoft Excel® or Word®, you may download the Sun Microsystems OpenOffice software for free at www.openoffice.org. This software includes Calc, a spreadsheet program with which you can fully utilize the Excel® file templates, and Writer, a word processing program that can access Word® files.

A QUICK REVIEW OF THE BASICS

1

The content of this book assumes that the reader already possesses a working knowledge of options and has experience writing covered calls on individual stocks and/or ETFs. Past experience writing uncovered puts would also be very beneficial, as it constitutes one of the two components of this option writing strategy.

This chapter will briefly summarize the essential terminology and features of options. Many of the words and phrases used in quotations are defined in the glossary. If more detailed background information is needed, either on the markets or on options, the reader is directed to the "Suggested Reading" in the Appendix.

WHERE ARE OPTIONS TRADED?

Option contracts are considered to be securities. As such, they are bought and sold through a brokerage firm. Either a full-service broker or a discount broker can be used, although option trades through a discount broker are usually much less expensive. Option contracts trade on U.S. securities exchanges, such as the Chicago Board Options Exchange (CBOE), the New York Stock Exchange (NYSE), the Philadelphia Stock Exchange (PHLX) and the Pacific Stock Exchange (PSE). The contracts traded on all of the exchanges are issued, guaranteed and cleared, that is to say settled or finalized, by the "Options Clearing Corporation

(OCC)." The OCC is a registered clearing corporation with the "Securities & Exchange Commission (SEC)." This provides you with needed protection to assure your transactions fit certain common standards and that they are all handled through an independent and unbiased third party.

THE OPTION BUYER

For purposes of this book, the "buyer" (also called "holder") of an "option" has the right to buy or sell shares either of individual stocks or ETFs for a specified price on or before a specific date. The specified price is termed the "strike price," and the specified date is called the "expiration date." A "call" is a right (but not the obligation) to *buy* the shares...like calling them away...while a "put" is a right (but not the obligation) of the option holder to *sell* the shares...like putting them into someone else's hands. The investor who purchases an option, whether it is a call or a put, is the option buyer. One "option contract," which defines the rights and obligations of the parties involved, is for 100 shares.

Thus, the buyer of XYZ October $40 calls has the right to purchase 100 shares of XYZ common stock per option contract for $40 per share through the October expiration date, which is always the third Saturday of the expiration month.

Similarly, the buyer of XYZ October $40 puts has the right to sell 100 shares of XYZ common stock per option contract for $40 per share through the October expiration date.

THE OPTION SELLER

Conversely, the investor who initiates a transaction by selling a call or put, or both, is the option "seller" or "writer" (which will be your side of the option transaction in all cases in this book).

The writer of XYZ October $40 calls would have the obligation to sell 100 shares of XYZ common stock per option contract for $40 per share through the option expiration date if a holder of such contracts decides to "exercise" the options and if "assignment" is made to the writer (a lottery process conducted by the option clearinghouse and the affected brokers). If assignment is made to the writer and the writer does not own the shares (as would be the case with uncovered call writing), he will be required to purchase the shares at the current market price, and sell them to the holder of the option at the strike price.

The writer of XYZ October $40 puts would have the obligation to purchase 100 shares of XYZ common stock per option contract for $40 per share, regardless of the current market price of the shares, through the option expiration date if a holder of such contracts decides to exercise the options and if assignment is made to the writer.

HOW A CALL OPTION BUYER PROFITS AND LOSES

The buyer of a call is speculating that the price of the "underlying security" will significantly *increase* soon. The price that the buyer pays to purchase the call is the "premium." If an upward price movement occurs in the underlying security, the buyer hopes to capitalize on an increase in value of the premium so that he can sell the option for a greater premium than he paid for it. Although other factors also come into play (such as the proximity of the call expiration date), the direction in price of a call option premium will *positively* track the direction in price of the underlying security. Thus, if the price of a stock is increasing, the price of calls for that stock will increase. If the price of a stock is decreasing, the price of its calls will decrease.

Let's assume that the current market price of XYZ shares is $37 ½ per share and that the current market price of the XYZ October $40 calls is $3 per contract. It would cost an investor $3,750 to acquire 100 shares of XYZ stock. But for $300 the investor can control 100 shares until October by purchasing one XYZ October $40 call contract (1 contract x $3 premium x 100 shares). If the price of XYZ stock should increase relatively quickly from $37 ½ to, say, $41, the market price of the call option would increase along with the stock, perhaps to a price of, say, $5 per contract. The option holder could then sell his option position at $5, realizing a $200 gain, a 66.6% investment return, in a relatively short period of time. Or he could continue to hold the position and face the prospect of additional gain or loss.

Had XYZ declined relatively quickly from $37 ½ to, say, $33, the market price of the call option would decrease with the stock, perhaps to a price of, say, $1 per contract. The option holder would then be faced with the decision of continuing to hold the position with the hope for a recovery in price and the risk of additional loss, or liquidating the position and realizing a $200 loss, or 66.6%.

HOW A PUT OPTION BUYER PROFITS AND LOSES

Similarly, the buyer of XYZ puts is speculating that the price of the underlying security will significantly *decrease* soon. If a downward price movement occurs in the underlying security, the buyer hopes to capitalize on an increase in value of the put premium so that he can sell the option for a greater premium than he paid for it. Although other factors also come into play (such as the proximity of the put expiration date), the direction in price of a put option premium will *negatively* track the direction in price of the underlying security. Thus, if the price of a stock is decreasing, the price of its puts will increase. If the price of a stock is increasing, the price of puts for that stock will decrease.

Let's again assume that the current market price of XYZ shares is $37 ½ per share and that the current market price of the XYZ October $35 puts is $3 per contract. An investor could initiate a "short sale" for 100 shares of XYZ stock, assuming all of the risks of such a transaction. But for $300 the investor can control 100 shares until October by purchasing one XYZ October $40 put contract (1 contract x $3 premium x 100 shares). If the price of XYZ stock should decrease relatively quickly from $37 ½ to, say, $34, the market price of the put option would increase with the decline in the stock, perhaps to a price of, say, $5 per contract. The option holder could then sell his option position at $5, realizing a $200 gain, a 66.6% investment return, in a relatively short period of time, or continue to hold the position and face the prospect of potentially additional gain or loss.

Had XYZ increased relatively quickly from $37 ½ to, say, $41, the market price of the put option would decline with the increase in the stock price, perhaps to a price of, say, $1 per contract. The option holder would then be faced with the decision of continuing to hold the position with the hope for a recovery in price and the risk of additional potential loss, or liquidating the position and realizing a $200 loss, or 66.6%.

HOW A CALL OPTION WRITER PROFITS AND LOSES

The writer (seller) of a call is an investor who is seeking to earn a premium that will represent a fixed return on investment. That investment is the amount of "margin" the investor is required to maintain in his brokerage account to support the call writing transaction, either in cash or securities acceptable to the broker. As the market for the underlying securities fluctuates, the amount of the margin requirement to support the uncovered call writing position changes at the end of each business day. Should the margin requirement exceed the amount of cash or securities on deposit, the investor will need to deposit additional cash or securities into the account within a specified period of time or the broker will generate the additional margin required by liquidating some or all of the investment positions in the account.

When an option seller initiates a new position by writing calls on a security he does not own (referred to by the broker as a "sell-to-open" or "uncovered call" transaction), the premium income is credited to his brokerage account the next business day following execution of the transaction. Again, the direction in price of a call option premium will *positively* track the direction in price of the underlying security. Thus, if the price of a stock is increasing, the price of calls for that stock will increase and the amount of margin requirement will increase. If the price of a stock is decreasing, the price of its calls will decrease and the margin requirement will correspondingly decrease.

Let's use the example of XYZ calls. The current market price of XYZ shares is $37 ½ per share and the current market price of the XYZ October $40 calls is $3 per contract. By selling one XYZ October $40 call contract, the writer will receive $300 into his brokerage account tomorrow (1 contract x $3 premium x 100 shares), less commissions. Even though the margin requirement will increase or decrease on a daily basis, if the option is held until the October expiration date and the market price of XYZ stock remains below $40 on that date, the call option will not be exercised (an option buyer would not pay $40 per share for stock he could buy on the open market for less). The writer keeps the entire premium and has no further obligation. The margin requirement is released, and the investor is able to write another option if desired.

If on the expiration date the market price of XYZ shares is above $40, the buyer will exercise the call option, in which case the writer's broker will purchase 100 shares of XYZ at the current market price to deliver to the buyer. The writer would incur a loss to the extent that the market price was greater than $43 (the writer received $3 per share of premium income and will receive $40 per share from the sale to the buyer at the strike price). If the market price of XYZ is between $40 and $43, the writer would have a net profit ranging from $0 to $300, depending on the specific price of the shares.

Prior to expiration, the market price of XYZ may increase beyond the strike price. If that occurred, the price of the option may well increase beyond the premium that was received when the call was written. This would result in an increased margin requirement. It is also possible that the option could be exercised prior to the expiration date if the market price of XYZ advanced beyond the strike price, however this is very uncommon. The buyer of a call would almost always sell his position in the open market before expiration rather than exercise the option. Therefore, when exercise of an option occurs it is typically on the expiration date.

If the price of XYZ stock should increase relatively quickly from $37 ½ to, say, $41, the market price of the call option would increase along with the stock, perhaps to a price of, say, $5 per contract. The option writer could then purchase back his option at $5 to close out his position, realizing a $200 (66.6%) investment loss. Or he could continue to hold the position and face the prospect of potentially additional gain or losses. Rather than face the uncertainty of a large loss, an investor should determine in advance the level at which the position would be purchased back and closed should the price of XYZ move significantly upward. This strategy is discussed in Chapter 4.

If XYZ declined relatively quickly from $37 ½ to, say, $33, the market price of the call option would decrease with the stock, perhaps to a price of, say, $1 per contract. The option writer could then, if desired, purchase the call to close the transaction at a gain of $200 (66.6%), or continue to hold the position, hoping to realize the entire $300 profit if the market price for XYZ remains below the $40 strike price on the expiration date.

HOW A PUT OPTION WRITER PROFITS AND LOSES

The writer (seller) of a put is an investor who is seeking to earn a premium that will represent a fixed return on investment. That investment is the amount of margin the investor is required to maintain in his brokerage account to support the put writing transaction, either in cash or securities acceptable to the broker. As the market for the underlying securities fluctuates, the amount of the margin requirement to support the uncovered put writing position changes at the end of each business day. Should the margin requirement exceed the amount of cash or securities on deposit, the investor will need to deposit additional cash or securities into the account within a specified period of time or the broker will generate the additional margin required by liquidating some or all of the investment positions in the account.

When an option seller writes puts (referred to by the broker as a "sell-to-open" or "uncovered put" transaction), the premium income is credited to his brokerage account the next business day following execution of the transaction. The direction in price of a put option premium will *negatively* track the direction in price of the underlying security. Thus, if the price of a stock is decreasing, the price of puts for that stock will increase and the amount of margin requirement will increase. If the price of a stock is increasing, the price of its puts will decrease and the margin requirement will correspondingly decrease.

Again, we will use the same example of an XYZ put. The current market price of XYZ shares is $37 ½ per share and the current market price of the XYZ October $35 puts is $3 per contract. By selling one XYZ October $35 put, the writer will receive $300 into his brokerage account tomorrow (1 contract x $3 premium x 100 shares), less commissions. Even though the margin requirement will increase or decrease on a daily basis, if the option is held until the October expiration date and the market price of XYZ stock remains above $35 on that date, the put option will not be exercised (an option buyer would not sell his shares for $35 when he could sell them on the open market for more). The writer keeps the entire premium and has no further obligation. The margin requirement is released, and the investor is able to write another option if desired.

If on the expiration date the market price of XYZ shares is below $35, the buyer will exercise the put option, in which case the writer's broker will purchase 100 shares of XYZ from the option holder at the $37 ½ strike price. The writer would have a paper loss on the acquired shares to the extent that the market price was less than $35 and a net loss on the entire transaction if the market price was less than $32 (the writer received $3 per share of premium income and will purchase the shares at the $35 strike price). If the market price of XYZ is between $32 and $35, the writer would have a gain ranging from $0 to $300, depending on the specific price of the shares.

Prior to expiration, the market price of XYZ may decline below the strike price. If that occurred, the price of the option may well increase beyond the premium that was received when the call was written. This would result in an increased margin requirement. It is also possible that the option could be exercised prior to the expiration date if the market price of XYZ declined below the strike price, however this too is very uncommon. The buyer of a put would almost always sell his position in the open market before expiration rather than exercise the option. Therefore, when exercise of an option occurs it is typically on the expiration date.

If the price of XYZ stock should decline relatively quickly from $37 ½ to, say, $33, the market price of the put option would increase in relationship to the decline in the stock, perhaps to a price of, say, $5 per contract. The option writer could then purchase back his option at $5 to close out his position, realizing a $200 (66.6%) investment loss. Or he could continue to hold the position and face the prospect of additional gains or losses. Rather than face the uncertainty of a large loss, an investor should determine in advance the level at which the position would be purchased back and closed should the price of XYZ move significantly downward. This strategy is also discussed in Chapter 4.

If XYZ increased relatively quickly from $37 ½ to, say, $41, the market price of the put option would decrease as the stock increased, perhaps to a price of, say, $1 per contract. The option writer could then, if desired, purchase the put to close the transaction at a gain of $200 (66.6%), or continue to hold the position, hoping to realize the entire $300 profit if the market price for XYZ remains above the $35 strike price on the expiration date.

As a seller, when you write both puts or calls on a security you receive the premiums paid by the buyers (less applicable brokerage commissions). The combined premium income is credited to your brokerage account the next business day following execution of the transactions. For uncovered put and call writers, the gain is limited to the amount of the premiums you receive. Your potential for loss is, as we shall see, theoretically unlimited...at least on the call side of the transaction. Hence the need for a plan of action to quickly control losses when they begin to occur.

As with stocks and ETFs, put and call options are "fungible." That is to say, all option contracts for the same underlying security with the same strike price and expiration date are identical and are interchangeable. For example, shares of XYZ common stock and the October $40 XYZ calls are both fungible. All XYZ common stock shares are the same and are interchangeable. All of the XYZ October $40 call contracts are the same and are interchangeable.

HOW STRIKE PRICES AND
EXPIRATION DATES ARE ESTABLISHED

Strike prices are established when the underlying shares either advance or decline to a certain price level and trade consistently around that level. Therefore volatile stocks and ETFs that trade in a broader range of prices would have more strike prices available for selection. There are typically a variety of strike prices available, some of which will usually be above the current market price of the shares and some of which will be below it.

Strike prices for options on most stocks and ETFs are normally set in $2 ½ or $5 increments, depending on the price of the underlying security. There are two notable exceptions to this: the PowerShares QQQ, which tracks the NASDAQ-100 Index, includes the 100 largest stocks listed on the NASDAQ, nicknamed the "Qs" or "Cubes" ("ticker symbol" QQQQ), and the Spiders Trust Series 1, which tracks the Standard & Poors® 500 Index (ticker symbol SPY). Strike prices on options for these ETFs are set in $1 increments both above and below the current market price, which gives the investor in these shares tremendous selection flexibility that is not otherwise available with most securities. Both the QQQQ and SPY are highly popular ETFs. They trade in huge volume and so do many of the option contracts associated with it.

There are also a variety of option expiration dates available that extend out as short as the current month to as long as three years for options on some stocks and ETFs. These very long-term options are referred to as "LEAPS," which stands for "Long-Term Equity Anticipation Securities." They are traded through your broker the same as other options and are available on many stocks. LEAPS have a January expiration date.

SELECTION OF STRIKE PRICES

Under this program you will write puts where the strike price of the options is *lower* than the current market price of the shares on which you are writing options and you will write calls where the strike price is *higher* than the price of the shares. This is referred to as being "out-of-the-money." To go back to our example, if the current price of shares you are interested in is $37 ½ and you write a put option with a $35 strike price, the option is said to be out-of-the-money by $2 ½. That is the difference between the market price of the shares when a put option is written and the strike price of the put option. Regarding the call side of the transaction, if you write a call option with a $40 strike price, the call would also be out-of-the-money by $2 ½.

If you were to write a put option with a strike price *higher* than the current price of the shares, the option is said to be "in-the-money." For example, if the current price of the shares is $37 ½ and you write a put option with a $40 strike price, the option is said to be in-the-money by $2 ½. You would receive a significantly higher premium by writing an in-the-money option when compared to an out-of-the-money option, but you are immediately placed into a situation where you would be required to purchase the shares at a higher price than they are currently trading if they remain above the strike price at expiration. If the price in this example remained the same until expiration, you would pay $40 for shares that are only worth $37 ½ at the time you wrote the option, or a loss of $2 ½ per share. However, due to the very large premium collected, it is still possible to realize a net gain (premium less "capital loss" on the shares). Similarly, if you write a $35 call when the shares are trading at $37 ½, you would be writing an in-the-money call. As with the in-the-money put, the premium you would receive would be greater, but you would be placed into the immediate position of having to sell short and deliver the shares at a market price to the call option holder at a strike price lower than the current market.

The program recommended in this book principally involves writing out-of-the-money puts and calls in order to earn premium income from both the put and the call as well as provide a range within which the underlying security can trade and remain profitable.

Finally, when the market price of the shares is the same as, or very close to, the strike price of an option, the option is said to be "at-the-money." An example of this would be if you were interested in writing a put or call option with a strike price of $37 ½ and the underlying shares were selling at $37 ½ per share, or within a nickel or so.

SHARE PRICE REMAINS BETWEEN
PUT AND CALL STRIKE PRICES AT EXPIRATION

It varies, but options experts say that on average for all option contracts about eighty-percent of the time options that are out-of-the-money when they are written expire without being exercised. This includes some contracts far out-of-the-money as well as those where the strike prices are closer to the market price, so it is difficult to generalize about specific contracts. If the expiration date comes and goes and the buyer does not exercise his put or call option, this means you have earned the premium and no further action is required. You can then write another put and call combination and collect additional premiums.

EXERCISE AND ASSIGNMENT
OF PUT AND CALL OPTIONS

You can anticipate that the call option holder will exercise his option (referred to as being "assigned") any time your option becomes in-the-money. This almost always occurs at expiration if the market price of the shares is higher than the strike price, although it could possibly happen at any time during the term of the option contract if the holder of the option wanted to exercise the right earlier. This would be unusual, as the option holder would typically sell his call option position rather than exercise the option prior to the expiration date. If an uncovered call is exercised and assigned to you, your broker would sell short the underlying shares at the current market value and deliver them to the option holder at the strike price specified in the call option contract you sold. Since the call would not be exercised unless the price of the shares were higher than the strike price, the transaction will place you in a loss position to the extent of the difference between the market price and the strike price times the number of contracts times 100 (the number of shares per contract). For example, if the strike price was $35, the market price on expiration was $38 and the number of contracts was 5, the loss would be $1,500 ($3 x 5 x 100). This would be offset by the call premium you received.

Likewise, you can anticipate that the put option holder will exercise his option causing the optioned shares to be put to you at the strike price, any time your option becomes in-the-money. This almost always occurs at expiration if the market price of the shares is lower than the strike price, although it could possibly happen at any time during the term of the option contract if the holder of the option wanted to exercise the right earlier. As with the call, this would be unusual. The option holder would typically sell his option position rather than exercise the option prior to the expiration date. Since the put would not be exercised unless the price of the shares were lower than the strike price, the transaction will result in a short-term unrealized (paper) loss for the put writer in the acquired shares to the extent of the difference between the market price and the strike price times the number of contracts times 100 (the number of shares per contract). For example, if the strike price was $35, the market price on expiration was $33 and the number of contracts was 7, the unrealized loss in the shares at the time of the transaction would be $1,400 ($2 x 7 x 100). Of course the shares may advance or decline from there. Your cost basis in the shares purchased would be reduced by the amount of put premium you received.

NO COMMISIONS PAID ON
NON-EXERCISED OPTION CONTRACTS

As a writer of put and call options, you pay an option commission when you initiate the transaction or close out a position by buying it back. If the options are not exercised and expire without value (out-of-the-money), as a put and call combination writer you keep the entire amount of both option premiums and pay no additional commissions at expiration. Of course, if you are required to purchase or sell short the shares at expiration to fulfill your obligation due to an assignment of a put or a call contract, then you would incur additional brokerage commissions.

ALL ABOUT MARGIN

2

Have you sent us an e-mail message yet requesting your Microsoft Excel® file templates? If you have not done so, please send an e-mail now to arrowpublications@cox.net requesting the "combinations files." You will find them a useful resource to assist in making decisions on which put and call option combinations to write once you have selected a specific stock or ETF to use for put and call combination writing. They will provide excellent information to simplify decision-making and save a good deal of time in "crunching the numbers."

MARGIN

For investors in the stock market, margin refers to buying stock or selling stock short on credit provided by the broker. Margin customers are required to keep securities on deposit with their brokerage firms as collateral for their borrowings. When writing uncovered put and call options, margin means the cash or securities required to be deposited by the option writer with the brokerage firm to support the uncovered writing transaction. Minimum margin requirements are currently imposed by the Board of Governors of the Federal Reserve System, the options markets and other regulatory organizations. Higher margin requirements may be imposed either generally or in individual cases by individual brokerage firms.

The calculation of your margin requirement is one of the more complicated aspects of uncovered put and call option writing. Fortunately the Excel® template does it all for you.

In this book we are using a method of margin calculation that is typical for the brokerage industry for uncovered writing on individual stocks and ETFs. It consists of three separate calculations each for the uncovered call and uncovered put, with the calculation resulting in the highest amount constituting the margin requirement. Your broker likely uses these same calculation methods, however the percentages applied in the calculations may vary from broker to broker. This is an important issue, and you should always determine how margin is calculated by any broker with whom you are considering trading. The Excel® template can be customized to apply your broker's percentages as long as they use the same calculation methodology. Some individual stocks that are considered riskier by the broker may require a greater margin than others that are not as risky. You should also find out from your broker what assets in your account are eligible to meet the margin requirement. This would typically include cash, government securities, other bonds, and unmargined stocks and ETFs.

Your broker recalculates the margin requirement each day after the market closes based upon the new closing price for the underlying security and the closing price for the put and call options that have been written. Again, the margin requirement for the combination is the larger of the three calculations for both the put and the call. If you do not have sufficient cash and/or securities on deposit in your account based on the new calculation on any given day, you will receive a "margin call" from your broker requiring the deposit of additional cash or securities into your account immediately to meet the new margin requirement. In the event you do not meet a margin call within the time constrictions imposed by your broker, assets in your account may be sold to meet the requirement.

After finishing the discussion on the rest of the worksheet we will outline different margin requirements in sample situations so you can get a better understanding of how the margin requirements work and how they change depending on price volatility. The following is the margin calculation methodology used in the "calculations" template, which are made automatically for you on the worksheet. We will review specific examples shortly.

Margin Calculation #1:
- 15% of the stock price
- Add the per share amount of the premium
- Multiply times 100 (the number of shares per contract)
- Multiply times the number of contracts written

Margin Calculation #2:
- 30% of the stock price (some brokerages have gone to 25%)
- Add the per share amount of the premium
- Subtract the amount by which the share price is out of the money
- Multiply times 100 (the number of shares per contract)
- Multiply times the number of contracts written

Margin Calculation #3:
- Multiply the number of option contracts by $1,000.

It was mentioned earlier that your broker may apply different percentages to the first two calculations, or a higher percentage may be applied to certain riskier stocks. If that is the case, the template can be customized to calculate your broker's margin requirements. In cell reference R5 insert the lower of the two percentages in your broker's calculations and in cell reference R6 insert the higher of the two percentages (the calculation that subtracts the out-of-the-money amount). You broker also likely sets a minimum dollar amount per contract (typically $1,000). If your broker uses a different number, it can be entered in cell reference R7. It is now adapted for your use. Be sure to save the file template.

UNCOVERED PUT WRITING

In order to begin our discussion on writing uncovered put and call combinations, we will examine the put and call segments of the combined transaction separately to identify the margin requirement for each component and the return on investment for each.

First we will focus on the put writing leg of the combination using an out-of-the-money put for Bed, Bath & Beyond shares. At the time the Excel® worksheet was prepared, the stock was trading at $39.15. Obviously there are a number of different strike prices and expiration dates that could have been selected, however, for purposes of this example, the $35 strike price was chosen with a June expiration date…a two-month option, since the worksheet was prepared in April. The portion of the "combinations" worksheet pertaining to the put side of the transaction is printed on the next page.

Bed, Bath & Beyond (BBBY) – Uncovered Put

PUTS										
x	x	x	x	x	x	x				%
SEC.	OPTION	EXPIR.	# OF	SECURITY	STRIKE		MARGIN	# OF	PREM.	ANNUAL
SYMBOL	SYMBOL	DATE	CONT.	PRICE	PRICE	PREM.	REQ.	DAYS	INCOME	RETURN
BBBY	BHQRG	18-Jun	10	$39.15	$35.00	$0.85	$10,000	60	$850	51.71%

The "bid" price for this option contract (the price a willing buyer is offering to pay) is $.80 and the "ask" price (the price a willing seller is offering to sell for) is $.90. For purposes of completing the Excel® worksheets, you should enter the approximate midpoint between the bid and ask prices for options you are considering, or perhaps slightly less if the spread is wider, in order to provide reasonable assurance that your order will be filled. Therefore, a price of $.85 has been entered. Keep in mind that for both puts and calls quoted under $3.00 the contracts trade in increments of 5 cents. For contracts priced over $3.00 the increment is 10 cents. Some actively traded option contracts trade in penny increments, especially where the strike price and the market price are very close.

The worksheet will automatically compute the highest margin requirement based on the three different methodologies of calculation. In this case, the three alternatives are computed as follows:

Margin Calculation #1:
- 15% of the stock price
    .15 x $39.15 = $5.8725
- Add the per share amount of the premium
    $5.8725 + $.85 = $6.7225

- Multiply times 100 (the number of shares per contract)
  $6.7225 x 100 = $672.25
- Multiply times the number of contracts written
  $672.25 x 10 = **$6,722.50**

Margin Calculation #2:
- 30% of the stock price
  .30 x $39.15 = $11.745
- Add the per share amount of the premium
  $11.745 + $.85 = $12.595
- Subtract the amount by which the share price is out of the money
  $12.595 - $4.15 = $8.445
- Multiply times 100 (the number of shares per contract)
  $8.445 x 100 = $844.50
- Multiply times the number of contracts written
  $844.50 x 10 = **$8445**

Margin Calculation #3:
- Multiply the number of option contracts by $1,000.
  10 x $1,000 = **$10,000**

The initial margin for the put side of the transaction would be $10,000, the largest of the three numbers.

The put writing portion of the combination indicates income of $850 for the two-month period and annualized return of 51.71% based on the initial margin requirement of $10,000.

UNCOVERED CALL WRITING

Next we will turn to the call writing leg of the combination using an out-of-the-money call for Bed, Bath & Beyond shares. Again, the market price of the stock is $39.15. As with the puts, there are a number of different strike prices and expiration dates that could have been selected. For purposes of this example, the $42 ½ strike price was chosen and the June expiration date.

Below is the portion of the "combinations" worksheet pertaining to the call side of the transaction.

Bed, Bath & Beyond (BBBY) – Uncovered Call

CALLS										
x	x	x	x	x	x	x				
SEC. SYMBOL	OPTION SYMBOL	EXPIR. DATE	# OF CONT.	SECURITY PRICE	STRIKE PRICE	PREM.	MARGIN REQ.	# OF DAYS	PREM. INCOME	% ANNUAL RETURN
BBBY	BHQFV	18-Jun	10	$39.15	$42.50	$1.20	$10,000	60	$1,200	73.00%

The bid price for this option contract (the price a willing buyer is offering to pay) is $1.10 and the ask price (the price a willing seller is offering to sell for) is $1.30. Therefore, a $1.20 price has been entered. Why is the premium for the call larger than the put premium? First, call premiums tend to be slightly higher than put premiums on average (although not always), as the overall bias of the market is to increase over time. In this case, however, the principal reason that the call premium is higher has to do with the price differential between the market price of the underlying stock and the strike price. In the put transaction the difference between the strike price and the market price is $4.15 ($39.15 - $35.) In the call transaction the difference is $3.35.

All other factors being equal (including the expiration date of the options), the closer an out-of-the-money option is to the strike price, the larger the premium when compared with other option alternatives.

Since the market price is closer to the strike price of the call option, this would account for most of the higher price of the premium. This makes logical sense, as the closer the market price is to the strike price, the greater the probability that it will increase beyond the strike price, with the option thereby becoming in-the-money and acquiring "intrinsic value." When it is out-of-the-money an option only has "time value." But when the market value exceeds the strike price in the case of a call, or declines below the strike price in the case of a put, the extent to which it becomes in-the-money is its intrinsic value. Example: If a call premium is $6, the strike price is $35 and the market price is $37, the intrinsic value portion of the premium is $2 ($37 - $35) and the time value portion is $4 ($6 - $2).

The worksheet will automatically compute the highest margin requirement for the call based on the three different methodologies of calculation. In this case, the three alternatives are computed as follows:

Margin Calculation #1:
- 15% of the stock price
      .15 x $39.15 = $5.8725
- Add the per share amount of the premium

$5.8725 + $1.20 = $7.0725
- Multiply times 100 (the number of shares per contract)
  $7.0725 x 100 = $707.25
- Multiply times the number of contracts written
  $707.25 x 10 = **$7,072.50**

Margin Calculation #2:
- 30% of the stock price
  .30 x $39.15 = $11.745
- Add the per share amount of the premium
  $11.745 + $1.20 = $12.945
- Subtract the amount by which the share price is out of the money
  $12.945 - $3.35 = $9.595
- Multiply times 100 (the number of shares per contract)
  $9.595 x 100 = $959.50
- Multiply times the number of contracts written
  $959.50 x 10 = **$9595**

Margin Calculation #3:
- Multiply the number of option contracts by $1,000.
  10 x $1,000 = **$10,000**

The initial margin for the call side of the transaction would be $10,000, the largest of the three numbers.

The call writing portion of the combination indicates income of $1,200 for the two-month period and annualized return of 73% based on the initial margin requirement of $10,000. The annualized return assumes you would write the same option every two months for the next year.

In addition to the three margin calculations described in this chapter, many brokerage firms assess an additional margin of $1,000 per contract on the first uncovered writing transaction open in your account, up to a maximum of $10,000. Thus, unless there were other open writing transactions, the writing of ten contracts (whether put or call) would increase the margin requirement by an additional $10,000 thereby making the total margin requirement $20,000. This extra margin, if it applies, should be entered in cell reference J24 on the "combinations" worksheet. This additional "first contract margin" would not apply to subsequent transactions that would be opened in the account. At such time as all open positions are liquidated, when a new uncovered write is initiated this first contract margin would again apply.

WRITING PUT AND CALL COMBINATIONS: WHAT IT IS AND HOW IT WORKS

You have seen a sample computation of the kind of return that is possible from separate out-of-the-money puts and calls on Bed, Bath & Beyond. Similar calculations for the margin requirement and the annualized return could be made for any stock or ETF on which options are offered. The projected return on investment, if realized, is significant for either the put writing or the call writing component alone.

Now it's time to take a look at the results that can be achieved with a put and call writing combination. We will first review the use of the "combinations" template, then look at the implications regarding margin requirement, return on investment, and then discuss strategies for success and risk assessment.

Let's begin by using the previous Bed, Bath & Beyond put and call writes, looking at them as our first writing combination.

USE OF THE "COMBINATIONS" TEMPLATE

What you see on the next page is how the "combinations" template format will appear when you bring up the file in Excel®. Multiple uses of this template by inputting different strike prices and expiration dates is the primary tool you will use in making specific combination writing selection decisions. Let's review how you would enter the data and the information that you would be given.

Bed, Bath & Beyond (BBBY) – Uncovered Put and Call Combination

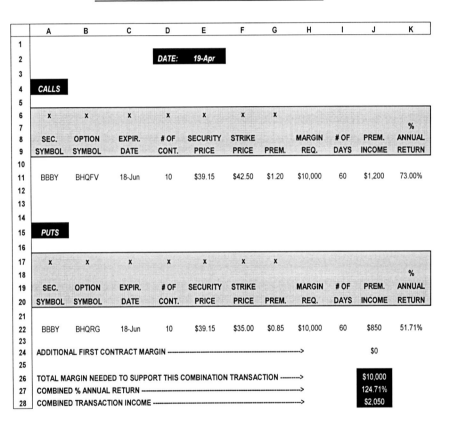

	A	B	C	D	E	F	G	H	I	J	K
1											
2				DATE:	19-Apr						
3											
4	CALLS										
5											
6	x	x	x	x	x	x	x				
7											%
8	SEC.	OPTION	EXPIR.	# OF	SECURITY	STRIKE		MARGIN	# OF	PREM.	ANNUAL
9	SYMBOL	SYMBOL	DATE	CONT.	PRICE	PRICE	PREM.	REQ.	DAYS	INCOME	RETURN
10											
11	BBBY	BHQFV	18-Jun	10	$39.15	$42.50	$1.20	$10,000	60	$1,200	73.00%
12											
13											
14											
15	PUTS										
16											
17	x	x	x	x	x	x	x				
18											%
19	SEC.	OPTION	EXPIR.	# OF	SECURITY	STRIKE		MARGIN	# OF	PREM.	ANNUAL
20	SYMBOL	SYMBOL	DATE	CONT.	PRICE	PRICE	PREM.	REQ.	DAYS	INCOME	RETURN
21											
22	BBBY	BHQRG	18-Jun	10	$39.15	$35.00	$0.85	$10,000	60	$850	51.71%
23											
24	ADDITIONAL FIRST CONTRACT MARGIN -->									$0	
25											
26	TOTAL MARGIN NEEDED TO SUPPORT THIS COMBINATION TRANSACTION -------->									$10,000	
27	COMBINED % ANNUAL RETURN -->									124.71%	
28	COMBINED TRANSACTION INCOME -->									$2,050	

Note rows 6 and 17 with the small "x"s in the first seven columns. This means you need to supply the information in the cells under those columns, both for the call writing transaction and the put writing transaction. For several columns (security symbol, expiration date, number of contracts, and security price), all you have to do is enter the data in the calls section and it will be duplicated in the puts section. If there is no "x" in a column, the information in that column is automatically calculated for you.

In Chapter 6 we will discuss in detail the easiest ways to gather the option symbol and premium quotation information needed to complete the worksheet.

INFORMATION YOU NEED TO ENTER INTO THE WORKSHEET

Security Symbol ("Sec. Symbol"): Many of the columns are obvious. Column A is the ticker symbol, in this case BBBY.

Option Symbol ("Option Symbol"): Column B is the ticker symbol for the option you are considering. This is important to have available for use when you decide to make a trade.

Expiration Date ("Expir. Date"): Column C is the option expiration date you are considering. This needs more detailed discussion. There are typically a wide variety of option expiration dates to choose from on most stocks and ETFs. Expirations were available on options for Bed, Bath & Beyond for the months of May, June, August, November, January, and the LEAPS for a year from that January…from the current month to over 21 months away. This gives investors quite a few choices to suit their own unique option writing needs. More detail will be provided shortly on how those selections are made, but at this point suffice it to say that you would often have quite a selection to choose from. For all stocks and ETFs, there is an assigned "option cycle" which means that generally there are options expiring the same four months every year plus at least the current and the next following month. Some stocks and ETFs also offer LEAPS.

There are three different cycles, and they are set as follows:

Cycle 1:	January	April	July	October
Cycle 2:	February	May	August	November
Cycle 3:	March	June	September	December

Bed, Bath & Beyond is Cycle 2. Regardless of which option cycle is assigned for any given security, there is always an option created with an expiration date for the current and the following month as well.

Enter the expiration date of the option you are considering, remembering to use the third Friday (the last day of trading before expiration) as the day of the month. You may wish to select several different expiration dates, using a separate copy of the worksheet for each date, to determine which expirations appear to be most attractive and that appear to meet your objectives.

Number of Contracts ("# Of Cont."): Column D is the number of put and call contracts you wish to write. An option contract always applies to one hundred shares, also called a "round lot." You cannot write an option contract for an "odd lot," which is less than one hundred shares. Therefore, the number of contracts you write must be in multiples of 100 shares. For example, 3 contracts represent 300 shares, 5 contracts 500 shares, and, in this example, the 10 contracts represent 1,000 shares. While contracts can be written for any multiple of 100 shares, the larger the number of contracts sold, the more cost efficiency there typically is in brokerage commissions on option trades. When writing put and call combinations, it is not required that the same number of contracts of both puts and calls be traded, however the most efficiency in the use of margin will be obtained when the same number of contracts are written for both puts and calls, as the highest margin requirement will be applied in any case.

Security Price ("Security Price"): The current share price for BBBY follows in column E.

Strike Price ("Strike Price") : The strike price in column F specifies the price at which the option buyer has the right to exercise the option. You should select one or more out-of-the-money puts and calls, using a separate copy of the worksheet for each strike price, to determine which strike price appears to be more attractive and which one best meets your objectives.

Premium ("Prem."): Column G is your final entry. Plug in the current quote for the option, which you will get from your broker (more about this will follow in Chapter 6). Sometimes there can be a significant spread, or variance, between the bid and ask prices that are quoted for options. The bid price is what a buyer is currently bidding or willing to pay to buy the contract. The ask price is what a seller is currently asking or willing to sell the contract for. Actual trading will usually take place between those two figures. As the seller of the put and call options, you want this number to be as high as possible. Generally it is best to take the bid and ask prices, add them together and divide by two to get the approximate midpoint. So, if the bid is $.65 and the ask is

$.75, use the midpoint of $.70, or perhaps even a little less for conservatism if the spread is wider, and plug that figure into the worksheet under the "Prem." column. This is the premium per share that you could reasonably expect to receive if you placed an order. Keep in mind that for option contracts quoted under $3.00 the contracts trade in increments of 5 cents. For contracts priced over $3.00 the increment is 10 cents. Again, some actively traded contracts trade in penny increments.

CALCULATIONS AUTOMATICALLY MADE FOR YOU ON THE WORKSHEET

The rest of the data on the worksheet are calculations that are made for you for purposes of analyzing alternatives so that you can make the best put and call combination writing decisions to suit your investment objectives. You will likely want to examine options having several different expiration dates and strike price alternatives. You can either print out the worksheets for comparison as you enter the data, or you may wish to save the file for each alternative on your hard drive to retrieve for comparison purposes. For example, if you are looking at Bed, Bath & Beyond options with a June expiration date, a $42 ½ call strike price and a $35 put strike price, you might name and save the file as "BBBY Jun $42.50 & $35" to differentiate it from other expiration date and strike price filenames you are saving.

Margin Required ("Margin Req."): Column H is the initial margin that you will be required to have in your account before you can execute this trade. You will recall that the worksheet separately calculates the margin requirement for the put and the call component based on the three different margin calculations, which you will find to the right of the worksheet data. It then enters the margin for the call in cell H11 and for the put in cell H22 (which is the same number in the case of the Bed, Bath & Beyond example we are using here). The larger of these two calculations is then entered into cell J26. The total margin requirement for the combination is $10,000. The requirement would be the same if only one of the two components were written instead of both.

Remember that some brokers also establish an additional margin requirement for the *first uncovered writing position*, but not for additional ones as long as there is at least one uncovered put or call writing position open. This is often an extra $1,000 per contract, up to a maximum of $10,000, *in addition* to the highest of the other margin calculations. In our example, if either the put or the call was the first transaction in the account, $10,000 should be entered in cell J24. Then the total margin requirement would be $20,000. You should check with your broker to see if you have to meet such an additional margin condition. If so, keep a mental note of it, as you will need to enter the amount on the worksheet at such times as it applies. The additional margin requirement will also affect the annual return.

Number of Days ("# Of Days"): Column I calculates the number of days from the date you are using the worksheet through the date of expiration you entered. So, for example, for the BBBY option expiring June 18 there are 60 days remaining from the date the worksheet was prepared through the last trading day.

Premium Income ("Prem. Income"): You will see the total premium income you would receive into your brokerage account the day after your order is executed under column J. The commissions obviously vary from broker to broker. You can customize your own template to accommodate the charges for your brokerage accounts by entering the appropriate information on the template to the right of the put calculation cells "R1" and "R2."

Percent Annual Return ("% Annual Return"): Column K calculates the annualized yield from the net premium based upon the initial margin requirement. It is annualized because investors are used to thinking about their returns that way. For example, if you are seeking a 12% annual return you would not likely say you want a one-percent return per month, because people just have not been taught to think that way.

CHANGING MARGIN REQUIREMENT

As we have said, your broker will adjust the margin requirement at the end of each business day based upon the changes in market price for the underlying security and the option premium. Since you are writing a put and call combination on the same underlying security, when these prices change the margin requirement will increase for one of the two legs and will decrease for the other. The calculation that results in the greatest number then becomes the new margin requirement. For example, let's assume that the market price of BBBY increased from $39.15 to $44 and, correspondingly, the price of the call increased from $1.20 to

$4.25 and the price of the put declined from $.85 to $.35. The result is as follows.

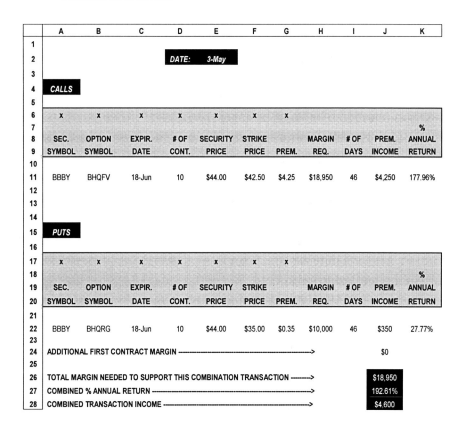

	A	B	C	D	E	F	G	H	I	J	K
1											
2				DATE:	3-May						
3											
4	CALLS										
5											
6	x	x	x	x	x	x	x				
7											%
8	SEC.	OPTION	EXPIR.	# OF	SECURITY	STRIKE		MARGIN	# OF	PREM.	ANNUAL
9	SYMBOL	SYMBOL	DATE	CONT.	PRICE	PRICE	PREM.	REQ.	DAYS	INCOME	RETURN
10											
11	BBBY	BHQFV	18-Jun	10	$44.00	$42.50	$4.25	$18,950	46	$4,250	177.96%
12											
13											
14											
15	PUTS										
16											
17	x	x	x	x	x	x	x				
18											%
19	SEC.	OPTION	EXPIR.	# OF	SECURITY	STRIKE		MARGIN	# OF	PREM.	ANNUAL
20	SYMBOL	SYMBOL	DATE	CONT.	PRICE	PRICE	PREM.	REQ.	DAYS	INCOME	RETURN
21											
22	BBBY	BHQRG	18-Jun	10	$44.00	$35.00	$0.35	$10,000	46	$350	27.77%
23											
24	ADDITIONAL FIRST CONTRACT MARGIN -->									$0	
25											
26	TOTAL MARGIN NEEDED TO SUPPORT THIS COMBINATION TRANSACTION -------->									$18,950	
27	COMBINED % ANNUAL RETURN -->									192.61%	
28	COMBINED TRANSACTION INCOME --->									$4,600	

Note that a $4.85 increase in the price of BBBY and a corresponding increase in the call option price from $1.20 to $4.25 results in an almost doubling of the margin requirement from $10,000 to $18,950. The margin requirement for the puts is still $10,000 (the third component of the margin calculation provides that the margin will always be at least $1,000 per contract). Thus, the new margin is the greater of the two numbers, or $18,950. It is always a good idea to have an additional cushion of cash or securities in your account to accommodate an increased margin requirement. Should it become insufficient, however, an immediate deposit of additional cash or securities would be required to avoid liquidation.

The investor would undoubtedly have liquidated the call position himself, and perhaps also his put, before the stock would have advanced to this point, as we will be discussing shortly. But this shows the impact of a significant change in the price of the underlying security on the margin requirement.

DOUBLE AND TRIPLE DIGIT
RETURNS ON INVESTMENT

In our original example of the BBBY options expiring on June 18, the annualized yield is calculated as if you could continue to write the same options at the same premium prices and with the same frequency--60 days to expiration--for an entire year, thereby realizing an annualized return from premium income on your margin requirement of 124.71%, before commissions. Obviously it is not going to occur that way, because the price of BBBY will change, and that means the price of the put and call options in the future will change as well. If you write another combination using the same underlying security, you may even select different strike prices, depending on the market value of the shares on the expiration date. But even though the annualized rate of return on subsequent writing opportunitics will diffcr from the return shown on the initial calculation, that is the best information we have at a given point in time, which is why it is used. Obviously we cannot predict where prices will be in the future, so we must use the measurements we have now.

That gives us the ability to compare one option opportunity with another (calculating the returns using different strike prices and expiration dates) in an "apples to apples" manner. Since your broker's margin requirement changes from day to day, the actual amount of cash or securities you need to have in your account at any given time to support that requirement may be less or more than the initial requirement.

Writing out-of-the-money put and call combinations can provide outstanding returns if the price of the underlying security remains relatively flat or increases or decreases within the range of the put and call strike prices from the time the options are written up to the expiration date. In these circumstances, the put writer's investment percentage return will significantly outperform the investor who simply owns the underlying security or the investor who only writes a put or call, but not both. Clearly there is also additional risk, as a combination presents the chance that either the put or the call position could move against you, resulting in a loss. This risk will be fully discussed shortly.

THE IMPACT OF STRIKE PRICE SELECTION

If you look separately at different strike prices for the put and the call components of the combination worksheet, the following becomes apparent:

When considering different out-of-the-money calls or puts with the same expiration date, the closer the market price of the underlying security is to the put or call strike prices, generally the larger the premium and the greater the annual return.

Let's see how this is true with the following examples:

DATE:	19-Apr									
CALLS										
x	x	x	X	x	x	x				%
SEC. SYMBOL	OPTION SYMBOL	EXPIR. DATE	# OF CONT.	SECURITY PRICE	STRIKE PRICE	PREM.	MARGIN REQ.	# OF DAYS	PREM. INCOME	ANNUAL RETURN
BBBY	BHQHH	20-Aug	10	$38.53	$40.00	$2.05	$12,139	123	$2,050	50.11%
BBBY	BHQHV	20-Aug	10	$38.53	$42.50	$1.15	$10,000	123	$1,150	34.13%
BBBY	BHQHI	20-Aug	10	$38.53	$45.00	$0.60	$10,000	123	$600	17.80%

Three different Bed, Bath & Beyond calls are considered above. The expiration date is the same for all of them, and obviously the price of the shares is the same. Three different strike prices have been selected, and the premiums, which have been obtained from a brokerage firm, are different as well. The $40 strike price, only $1.47 higher than the market price of the shares, has the greatest premium. Next is the $42 ½ strike price, which is $3.97 higher, with a premium of $1.15. Finally, the $45 strike price is $6.47 out-of-the-money, and has a premium of $.60. Note that the margin calculation is greater for the $40 strike price call option (the second formula for calculating margin results in a greater margin requirement when the strike price and the market price are closer together). Despite the larger margin requirement for the $40 call, the annualized return is still greater than the other option alternatives.

The larger premium for the closer strike price makes sense when you consider the perspective of the call *buyer*. If the buyer purchases the Bed, Bath & Beyond $40 strike price call, the share price needs to increase less to reach the strike price (at which point it becomes in-the-money and starts to build intrinsic value) than if he had purchased the $42 ½ or the $45 call. Therefore, he would expect to pay more for the call which has a strike price closer to the market price. As the call writer, you would expect a greater return on the $40 call than on the $42 ½ call (50.11% vs. 34.13%), since you would have a smaller range for the market price of the stock before your call would be in-the-money.

We will find the same trend in regard to several different put option alternatives that have the same expiration date. Again, three different strike prices have been selected with differing premiums.

					DATE:	19-Apr					
PUTS											
x	x	x	x	x	x	x					%
SEC.	OPTION	EXPIR.	# OF	SECURITY	STRIKE		MARGIN	# OF	PREM.	ANNUAL	
SYMBOL	SYMBOL	DATE	CONT.	PRICE	PRICE	PREM.	REQ.	DAYS	INCOME	RETURN	
BBBY	BHQTU	20-Aug	10	$38.53	$37.50	$2.05	$12,579	123	$2,050	48.36%	
BBBY	BHQTG	20-Aug	10	$38.53	$35.00	$1.20	$10,000	123	$1,200	35.61%	
BBBY	BHQTZ	20-Aug	10	$38.53	$32.50	$0.65	$10,000	123	$650	19.29%	

The $37 ½ strike price, only $1.03 lower than the market price of the shares, has the greatest premium. Next is the $35 strike price, which is $3.53 lower, with a premium of $1.20. Finally, the $32 ½ strike price is $6.03 out-of-the-money, and has a premium of $.65. Note that the margin calculation is greater for the $37 ½ strike price call option (again, the second formula for calculating margin results in a greater margin requirement when the strike price and the market price are closer together). Despite the larger margin requirement for the $37 ½ call, the annualized return is still greater than the other option alternatives.

As with the call, the larger premium for the closer strike price makes sense when you consider the perspective of the put *buyer*. If the buyer purchases the Bed, Bath & Beyond $37 ½ strike price put, the share price needs to decline less to reach the strike price (at which point it becomes in-the-money and starts to build intrinsic value) than if he had purchased the $35 put. Therefore, he would expect to pay more for the put which has a strike price closer to the market price. As the put writer, you would expect a greater return on the $37 ½ put than on the $35 put (48.36% vs. 35.61%), since you would have a smaller range for the market price of the stock before your put would be in-the-money.

THE IMPACT OF EXPIRATION DATE SELECTION

In addition to strike price selection, choosing an expiration date is the other decision the put and call combination writer faces. There is one thing that can *always* be said regarding expiration dates:

> *When considering different puts with the same strike price or calls with the same strike price, whether in-the-money or out-of-the-money, there is always an upward progression in the price of a put or call option premium as the length of the time to expiration increases.*

This will always be the case for this reason: if you are comparing options with various expirations using the same strike price, it makes sense that if you were a *buyer* of a put or a call option you would be willing to pay more for one expiring in August than you would be for one expiring three months earlier in May. That is because with the August contract the buyer has three more months for the shares to possibly go down (for a put) or up (for a call) so he can profitably sell his option contract or exercise it at expiration. And as an option *writer*, you would need to be prepared to accept a longer period of investment risk in exchange for a larger premium and locking in your potential return for a longer period of time.

Let's look at several calculations using different expiration dates for three different Bed, Bath & Beyond call and put options:

DATE: 19-Apr

CALLS

SEC. SYMBOL	OPTION SYMBOL	EXPIR. DATE	# OF CONT.	SECURITY PRICE	STRIKE PRICE	PREM.	MARGIN REQ.	# OF DAYS	PREM. INCOME	% ANNUAL RETURN
BBBY	BHQEV	21-May	10	$38.53	$42.50	$0.30	$10,000	32	$300	34.22%
BBBY	BHQHV	20-Aug	10	$38.53	$42.50	$1.15	$10,000	123	$1,150	34.13%
BBBY	BKQKV	19-Nov	10	$38.53	$42.50	$2.00	$10,000	214	$2,000	34.11%

DATE: 19-Apr

PUTS

SEC. SYMBOL	OPTION SYMBOL	EXPIR. DATE	# OF CONT.	SECURITY PRICE	STRIKE PRICE	PREM.	MARGIN REQ.	# OF DAYS	PREM. INCOME	% ANNUAL RETURN
BBBY	BHQQG	21-May	10	$38.53	$35.00	$0.30	$10,000	32	$300	34.22%
BBBY	BHQTG	20-Aug	10	$38.53	$35.00	$1.20	$10,000	123	$1,200	35.61%
BBBY	BHQWG	19-Nov	10	$38.53	$35.00	$1.95	$10,000	214	$1,950	33.26%

It can be seen that for both puts and calls, the longer the time to the expiration date, the larger the option premium.

You can examine the premium income, margin and annualized return calculations for puts and calls with different strike prices and expiration dates by multiple uses of the "combinations" template to view the projected returns.

DECAYING OF OPTION PREMIUMS OVER TIME

As the number of days increases to expiration, *the rate of increase* in the amount of the premium tends to slow down. Accordingly, many option combination writers prefer to stick with the shorter term expiration writing opportunities. The time value component of an option premium (the amount by which it is out-of-the-money) gradually decays over the life of the option. The rate of decay in the option price accelerates as the time to expiration draws nearer, so time decay often tends to work in favor of option writers who write shorter term contracts. Shorter term put and call options, while often providing the writer with more premium dollars of income per day until expiration and therefore a higher annualized investment return, will however not give you as much downside protection as longer-term options, since the premium is always larger for longer term options. So, the proper selection of an expiration date is dependent on your beliefs about the near-term direction of the market, just as is strike price selection.

Assume for a moment that the price of the underlying BBBY shares remains exactly the same during the entire period until the put and call options that were written in April expire out-of-the-money in November. This obviously will never happen, but will help make an important point. Since the time value of options is a decaying asset, one might expect that the price of the options would decline pro-rata in a straight line progression day by day over their life until they expire without value on the expiration date…like this.

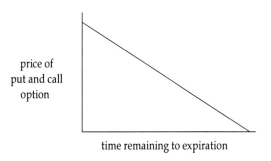

price of
put and call
option

time remaining to expiration

That is not typically the way things work, however. Usually the time value of an option retains more of its value until it gets closer to the expiration date. Thus, if BBBY's stock price were to remain exactly the same, for a seven month put and call option, for example, the decay in the price of the options as they get closer and closer to the date of expiration might look something more like this.

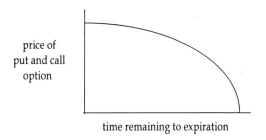

price of
put and call
option

time remaining to expiration

As you can see, with a flat price for BBBY the options, even though they are slowly decaying in value over the early months, hold more of their value until closer to expiration. An option writer could take some advantage of this by writing one or two month contracts and then buying back the puts and calls to close just before expiration, say when the price of the options are only a small fraction of the original price when they were written. It would not cost too much to buy them back at this time, and then the investor can write a new combination at a higher premium with another one or two month time period to the next expiration. This may provide a greater return than if the investor had simply waited for the first options to expire. The primary disadvantage of doing this is that the investor will pay additional commissions when the options are bought to close, which increases the overall cost. That is the reason why holding out-of-the-money options until expiration is usually recommended. Some brokers, however, reduce their commission costs for option trades when the price of the option premium is very low, which helps investors desiring to buy-to-close and initiate new positions.

SHORT-TERM VS. LONG-TERM PUT AND CALL WRITING

What, in summary, are the advantages of writing shorter-term options versus the advantages of writing longer-term options? Let's do an assessment:

Advantages of writing shorter-term puts and calls

- For puts, less likelihood of shares being put to you at expiration because there is less time for the price to go down below the strike price.

- For both puts and calls, due to the shortness of time, less likelihood of the underlying security moving against you resulting in having to buy back your position(s) at a loss.
- Greater return on investment, given the time period of the transaction and the phenomenon that option prices decay most rapidly during the months closest to expiration.
- For investors seeking to purchase the underlying shares at a discount to the current market price through put writing, there is a greater opportunity to purchase the underlying shares at a lower price, as you may be able to reduce the strike price in future put writing selections if the share price declines gradually but does not reach your strike price at expiration.

Advantages of writing longer-term puts and calls

- Larger total premiums that you will receive.
- Less brokerage commissions, because you will not be writing new contracts as often. If you were writing only one month options, you would incur three times the brokerage commissions compared with writing options with three month expirations.
- More downside protection in the event the price of the underlying shares passes your strike price, since the premium is greater on longer-term options.
- Less administrative work, since you only have to research option writing opportunities, handle trades and do recordkeeping as options expire.
- Ability to do some tax planning by selecting options that expire in the next tax year (more in Chapter 7).

Your broker may allow you to select different expiration dates for the put and call components of your option writing combination and still be subject to only one margin requirement. It is best, however, to utilize the same expiration dates for both legs of the combination. If you have different expiration dates for the puts and the calls, when the earliest expiration date occurs this could cause some awkwardness in selecting a suitable option expiration date for new options to replace the expiring ones. It is best that both legs of the combination either expire at the same time or that they are bought to close at the same time so that all new transactions can have maximum flexibility and not be encumbered. It can also be confusing if you have differing expiration dates within the same combination when you are writing combinations on numerous underlying securities. For purposes of this program it is assumed that for any given option writing combination, both the put and the call component will have the same expiration date.

Having addressed the mechanics of put and call combination writing through the use of the "combinations" template, we are faced with the issue of how to earn consistent money with this investment technique...enough money to warrant the additional risk we will be taking as combination writers. To bring this to conclusion, we now need to formulate a consistent plan that we will automatically follow.

BENEFITS, RISKS AND A
COMBINATION WRITING STRATEGY

Before we attempt to develop a workable strategy for combination writing, let's identify the rewards and the risks of the combination writing investment program so we can weigh them against each other as we formulate our strategy.

Benefits:

1. **Additional income** – Writing a combination of put and call options can provide an ongoing stream of premium income from two sources utilizing the same margin requirement (in effect, "two for the price of one"). This double option writing income can significantly enhance total returns in a flat, slower growth or modestly declining stock market.

2. **Income paid up-front** – Unlike most investments, the income received from put and call writing is credited to your brokerage account the next business day, creating immediate cash flow. If this up-front income is reinvested it can serve to enhance the overall return on the original investment.

3. **Opportunity to purchase stock at a lower price** – Unlike uncovered calls, puts can be written with two potential purposes in mind: (1) the desire to simply earn premium income from the put writing activity; and (2) the desire, or

at least willingness, to acquire the underlying shares at the strike price if the market price on the expiration date is below the strike price. Your objective may incorporate one or both of these purposes.

4. **Predetermined return** – The investment return you receive from put and call combination writing can be evaluated prior to initiating the investment positions by using the "combinations" template. You will know what the put and call writing income will be, how much in cash or securities you will be required to maintain in your account when the options are initially written and, in the case of puts, the investment you will need to make in the underlying shares if the market price falls below the strike price at expiration and you elect to buy the shares instead of buying back your put position to close. When we complete the development of a strategy, you will also have a better concept of your downside risk of loss.

5. **Fungibility and ease of trading** – Exchange-listed options, as with individual stocks and ETFs, are fungible. That is, each listed option is interchangeable with any of the same listed option contracts. This enables investors to initiate and, if desired, close out a position in the open market at any time through their brokerage account rather than potentially face having the options exercised at expiration. Fungible option contracts became available in 1973. Since options are actively traded on the open market, put and call option transactions can usually be executed as easily as trading stocks and ETFs.

Risks:

1. **Exposure to the stock market** – Writing put and call options means that the investor is subject to stock market risk, as the performance of both the put and the call contracts is tied to the price movement of the underlying securities. Should the uncovered put writer be required to purchase the shares, their price could continue to decline, resulting in investment losses. For the uncovered call writer, the potential for loss is theoretically unlimited. If the underlying share price on which calls are written advances above the strike price, the writer faces the prospect of having to either (1) buy back the calls prior to close, most likely at a loss; or (2) having the calls exercised at the expiration whereby the writer's broker would sell shares short at the higher current price to deliver the shares to the call holder at the lower strike price, thereby putting the writer in a loss position. The writer would remain at risk in a short position until the position was closed out. All of this dictates disciplined loss limitation practices, which will be a key consideration as we develop our overall combination writing strategy.

2. **Limited gain opportunity in relation to the potential for loss** – An option writer's potential gain on the option transactions is limited to the amount of put and call writing premium income received. Depending on the strike prices selected and the extent of a rise or fall in the underlying shares prior to the expiration date, the losses incurred could significantly exceed the amount of premium income received before the positions are closed.

3. **Unanticipated exercise of options** – The holder (buyer) of a put option has the right, but not the obligation, to exercise the option to sell his shares subject to a put contract and to purchase shares subject to a call contract at the strike price at any time through the expiration date. A writer can expect that his put and call contracts will rarely, if ever, be subject to assignment if the market price of the shares is between the strike prices of the put and call option contracts written. If, however, the market price falls below the put strike price or rises above the call strike price, it is possible that the holder could exercise the options at any time, thus requiring the option writer to purchase the underlying shares at the strike price (for puts) or sell the shares short at the current market price for delivery at the strike price (for calls) before the expiration date. Exercise of options generally occurs at the expiration date, and then usually only if the market price falls below the strike price for puts or rises above the strike price for calls. On occasion, however, a holder may decide, for whatever reason, to exercise an option prior to the expiration date, which obligates the writer of options that are assigned to fulfill the terms of the option contracts immediately.

4. **Potential lack of option market liquidity** – Option contracts generally trade in much smaller quantities than common stock or ETF shares. Options for some stocks and ETFs are very actively traded. Others trade very few contracts. This may cause the bid and ask price spread to widen significantly. For this reason, investors are generally encouraged to place limit orders (see Glossary) with their brokers on option trades instead of market

orders to eliminate the risk of an order being filled at a different price than what a current quote might indicate. Market orders can be placed for very actively traded options where the spread between bid and ask is very small.

5. **Possibility of a decrease in option premiums** – The price of option premiums are determined by market forces and mathematical models. During periods of market volatility, option premiums tend to be larger than during periods of stable markets. It is difficult to predict future volatility. Should markets become less volatile, or should stocks be less attractive to investors in the future, it is possible that option premiums may not be as large as they have been in the past. Such an occurrence would tend to make the returns from put and call combination writing less attractive than they have been during periods of larger option premiums.

6. **Commissions on option trades** – The commissions charged by full-service brokers and discount brokers vary significantly. It is important for the investor to find a broker, whether discount or full-service, where commission costs can be minimized.

The first two risks identified, which are related, are the most potentially damaging for the combination writer. Accordingly, they will be addressed carefully as we now develop our plan for successful put and call writing combinations.

UNCOVERED CALL WRITING RISK

Protecting yourself from risk when writing uncovered calls is an entirely different proposition than avoiding risk when writing uncovered puts. With puts, you simply find a stock or ETF that you would be happy to own for the long-term at a discounted price. You then write puts at a strike price at which you are prepared to purchase the underlying shares. If the share price remains above the strike price, you have achieved your return objective. If the price of the shares goes below the strike price, you have achieved your return objective on the option write, and you have also purchased shares for less money than you would have paid had you bought them at the time you initiated the put transaction. You have no such double-positive opportunity when writing uncovered calls. You only have the additional premium income you receive for a single margin requirement. As the mirror image of writing puts, if the underlying shares remain below the strike price, you have achieved your return objective. However, if the shares advance above the strike price, you are faced with the possibility of having to close out your call position (buy-to-close) before the expiration date, depending on the amount by which the shares advance above the strike price and the time value portion of the option premium remaining until expiration. If you hold your position until expiration and the market price of the shares goes above the strike price, you will undoubtedly have to sell the shares short at the higher market price to deliver to the option buyer at the lower strike price. To the extent that the market price of the shares is greater than the call strike price by the combined put and call option premiums, you will be in a loss position on the combination transaction.

MITIGATING RISK WHEN
WRITING UNCOVERED CALLS

Assuming you do not wish to risk having to sell shares short, how do you protect yourself from undue risk on the uncovered call component? There are two key practices that can mitigate the risk to more acceptable levels.

Practice #1: Avoid any security that is likely to increase substantially in value during the time period of a proposed uncovered call write. One merely needs to think about the situations in which stocks go up in value to realize what must be avoided. They would include the following:

(1) Avoid stocks that have any reasonable prospect of being acquired and thereby tacking on significant value as a result of a bid by another company.

(2) Avoid stocks that are likely to have prospects of significant positive news that could move the share price upward.

(3) Consider utilizing ETFs instead of individual stocks so that if such circumstances as described above occur to a company that is part of an ETF portfolio the effect is diluted since it is only one of a number of stocks contained within that portfolio.

Practice #2: Establish a clear exit strategy that you will use on all of your uncovered call writes so that you know *in advance* what action you will take if the underlying security increases to the point where losses are being incurred.

Let's discuss each of these two practices. For the first practice, we can all readily think of the names of many stocks that might be subject to acquisition. While not only small companies get acquired, certainly there is a far greater likelihood that a small technology company could be acquired than a company such as IBM. One could write uncovered calls forever and likely never worry that IBM would be acquired at a huge premium price. So, avoid like the plague writing uncovered calls on any stock that even has the appearance of being acquired at a premium.

Although not as easy, we should also be able think of companies that might be likely to experience positive earnings surprises or other positive news. Again, the example of IBM is appropriate. If IBM grew its earnings by 5%, it would be the equivalent of creating a new Fortune 500 company. So, significant upside surprises are far more likely to occur in smaller companies. A small to medium sized biotechnology company conducting trials for a new drug that might cure a form of cancer comes immediately to mind. If there were an announcement that such a trial had been successful, it could trigger an immediate and substantial rise in the share price. Any successful new or improved product offering could propel a small company's stock price higher. Witness the short-term price movement years ago of Boston Scientific when it received approval in the US and internationally for its new drug-coated stent that would compete with Johnson & Johnson.

Also consider the impact of a positive announcement to a small company. For example, while the discovery of a cure for Alzheimer's disease would undoubtedly have a positive effect on the stock price for Pfizer, the largest ethical drug company in the world, imagine the impact such a discovery would have on a small to medium sized company. Sticking with larger companies cannot absolve you from upside risk, but it can at least help you sleep better at night. It is also a good idea to avoid having open uncovered call positions when a company reports earnings, especially if the company has not provided earnings guidance.

Finally, we have discussed the many advantages of ETFs in relation to individual stocks and mutual funds. ETFs are more broadly diversified than individual stocks, but some have a significantly larger number of underlying stocks in their portfolios than others. By choosing an ETF that contains a substantial number of stocks, if very positive news or an offer to acquire is issued with respect to one of the companies contained in the ETF, the effect will be far more dilutive than if you owned the stock subject to the positive or acquisition news. While the ETF containing such a stock may well rise, the increase will be far more muted than would be the case by owning the subject stock.

The second practice simply means that you may be in no frame of mind to make a decision about when to cut your losses short if they have already started to occur. Shortly we will offer several pre-planned strategies to utilize on all put and call writing combinations when the price of the underlying security goes against you to the point where losses are being incurred. Please read those carefully. Not having an exit strategy is a prescription for disaster when the event occurs.

FIVE KEY QUESTIONS

Our plan of action will be based on resolving the answers to five important questions:

- What individual stocks and/or ETFs will serve us best as underlying securities in our combination writing activity?

- What should the price differential be between the strike prices and the market prices of the underlying securities for combination writing?

- Which put and call option expiration dates will serve us best in our combination writing?

- At what point should action be taken if the market price of the underlying security moves toward, or past, the put or the call strike price and losses begin to occur?

- How many uncovered option combination contracts can I write before I potentially become overextended?

The answer to these questions has a lot to do with the risk we are willing to assume as investors. The risks of put and call option combination writing go well beyond the risks that investors take who simply write covered calls or only uncovered puts. Therefore, as we try to answer the above questions, the discussion of setting investment objectives and willingness to accept investment risk should be the keys to establishing our strategy.

SETTING INVESTMENT OBJECTIVES

While all investors would like to reach the highest possible returns, there is always a clear tradeoff between risk and reward. The degree of risk any investor is prepared to take is a very personal matter, as described in the following investment scenarios in progressive order of risk taking:

- An investor who has always kept his resources in bank certificates of deposits, Treasury bills or short-term Treasury notes might well lose sleep if he invested money in a broad based equity mutual fund, Exchange Traded Fund or long-term Treasury or corporate bonds.

- An investor who sleeps well owning ETFs may lose sleep if he switches to a portfolio of individual stocks.

- An investor who sleeps peacefully writing covered calls on his stock and ETF portfolio may readily lose sleep if he were to begin writing uncovered puts, even if he were to write them on the same underlying stocks.

- And the put writer, who sleeps well knowing that he may have the opportunity to buy a stock at a discount with his strategy, may lie sleepless with the thought of potential losses in either a strong up or down market if he initiates a put and call combination writing program.

No doubt we could add other examples to these. So an investor's willingness to assume risk is clearly a relative and highly personal matter...one that only you as an individual investor can answer for yourself. If you are an investor who is willing to try taking on greater risk for greater returns, perhaps the best course of action is to advance from wherever you are to the next level of risk and see how well you sleep. If you can, at some point you may wish to advance to the next level, and so on. When you get to the level where you lose sleep over it, back off to the highest level where you were able to sleep comfortably and use that strategy for your at-risk investment funds unless your comfort level changes. While there is a bit of tongue-in-cheek in this, there is also an element of truth in it. As investors we do need to take some level of risk to achieve an acceptable rate of return.

Fundamental to your decision on how much risk you are willing to take is determining how much return you wish to try to achieve...establishing your investment objectives. While all investors should have a combination of equity, fixed income and cash investments, we are addressing here only the equity and higher risk portion, however much that portion might be.

As we have seen from the previous combination writing examples with Bed, Bath & Beyond, even by selecting puts and calls for writing that are well out-of-the-money, it is possible to achieve double-digit, and sometimes triple-digit, annualized investment returns on our investment capital. If that were achievable, most investors would likely not want to take any additional risk, as such returns would exceed those of most investors' wildest imaginations. Since all risk is relative, the program of option combination writing we propose in this book could be referred to as "conservative high risk." While on the surface this would appear to be an oxymoron, it should make more sense as we fully describe it.

CONSERVATIVE HIGH RISK COMBINATION WRITING

First Question: What individual stocks and/or ETFs will serve us best as underlying securities in our combination writing activity?

There is a three-part answer to this question. The first part deals with comfort, the second with diversification, and the third part with volatility.

Comfort

Let's consider the first part...comfort. Foremost and above all, you should *never* choose an underlying security for combination writing that you would not be comfortable owning for the long term. It is always possible that you could end up owning the shares if the put option side of the combination were exercised and assigned to you. Some option writers look for securities that offer large put and call premiums and then write uncovered options on them to maximize profit potential. Such an approach is fraught with danger. If you are compelled to purchase shares due to assignment of puts, you will sleep much more comfortably knowing you have bought shares that have fundamental underlying value. This applies to both individual stocks and ETFs. Therefore, always seek out securities with which you are very comfortable and then look for option writing opportunities on those securities.

Diversification

As an investor you may or may not be comfortable with Apple, Inc. (ticker symbol AAPL) and the PowerShares QQQ that tracks the NASDAQ-100 Index, ETF (ticker symbol QQQQ). Due to their prominence, however, they will serve as good examples for discussion purposes. Apple, by the way, in addition to trading on its own on the NASDAQ, is one of the 100 stocks that comprise the QQQQ. What we want to do is to assess the risk from a diversification standpoint of writing uncovered put and call combinations on Apple vs. the QQQQ. Let's assume that you would be comfortable with both of these securities. If you were going to write combinations on one of them, what are the issues regarding diversification?

First we will consider Apple. It is trading at $140 when you enter the data onto your worksheet. You decide that you will write a combination 2-month put with a $110 strike price and a 2-month call with a $170 strike price, giving you about $30 room in either direction before your option would be in-the-money and susceptible to exercise at expiration. The day following the execution of the transactions you receive the premiums in your account, which you will keep in their entirety as long as the market price remains within the $110 to $170 price range at expiration. But what would happen to Apple's stock if one week later the corporate headquarters of the company burned to the ground, with CEO Steve Jobs and several other top executives killed in the fire? Quite likely the stock would trade below your put strike price and may continue to do so at expiration, resulting in the assignment of your options so that you own the shares. You would be faced with a substantial paper loss (or a realized loss if you bought back the put contracts to close prior to expiration). On the other hand, what if Microsoft Corporation, with its $70 billion in cash, decided to make a tender offer for Apple at a price substantially higher than the current market price? The stock would mushroom in price, likely well beyond your call strike price, creating the probability that your call options would be assigned. If they were, you would have to sell short an equivalent number of shares on the open market at the prevailing market price to deliver to the buyer at the $170 strike price, putting you in a substantial loss position.

Now let's consider the QQQQ. It is trading at $36 when you enter the data onto your worksheet. You decide that you will write a combination 2-month put with a $31 strike price and a 2-month call with a $41 strike price (unlike most securities, strike prices are offered on the QQQQ in $1 increments), giving you about $5 room in either direction before your option would be in-the-money and susceptible to exercise at expiration. The day following the execution of the transactions you receive the premiums in your account, which you will keep in their entirety as long as the market price remains within the $31 to $41 price range at expiration. Now let's assume that the exact same negative and positive events would occur with Apple as described on the previous page. What is the impact on your combination writing position on the QQQQ? Since Apple is only one of one hundred of the stocks composing the QQQQ, the impact is substantially tempered when compared with direct ownership in Apple. Furthermore, ironically Microsoft is also one of the securities comprising the QQQQ, so if it would decline as Apple advances on the announced tender offer, the net effect would be greatly muted. Whether the price of the QQQQ would be driven either below the put strike price or above the call strike price is impossible to say, but one thing can be said with absolute certainty...the diversified position by writing puts and calls on an underlying security owning 100 different stocks substantially insulates you in comparison with combination writing on a single security.

You may make the case that such dramatic events are extremely rare or highly unlikely. This is true, but these are only two examples of many different things that could occur to drive the stock price of any individual security substantially up or down. We have seen the market price of individual stocks decline by double-digits in a single day when an earnings shortfall is reported by a company. We have also seen double-digit increases in a single day on positive earnings surprises, or on positive news, such as an acquisition or when a biotechnology company receives FDA approval for a new drug. When you add up all of the opportunities for positive and negative news, clearly there is substantial comfort to be gained by writing combinations on a security such as an ETF that contains many stocks within a broad market index or a sector that appeals to you. The best world for you if you are writing combinations is that there is no significant good news or bad news. This would help keep the price of your underlying security within the put and call strike price range, which will maximize your profit. However, if there is market driving news, whether positive or negative, about a specific security, you will clearly be better off having written option combinations on a diversified ETF than an individual stock.

For your information, you will find in the Appendix a partial list of ETFs currently available on which put and call options can be written, the ticker symbols, and the category to which each belongs. You are encouraged to do additional research on this list to determine if some of these securities may be consistent with your objectives. When you request the "combination files" by e-mail, we will also send you an Excel® template containing a list of all currently traded U.S. ETFs along with related information. ETFs offer participation in the broad market, industry sectors, regions, investment styles, or international. More information about each specific ETF can be obtained online at the NASDAQ Web site (www.nasdaq.com) or the Bloomberg.com Web site (www.bloomberg.com) by clicking on their "ETFs" tabs. Unless you have the resources to diversify your combination writing with many individual stocks, you should strongly consider the use of ETFs to easily achieve such diversification.

Volatility

Finally, we turn to the subject of volatility. To do so we need to examine the issue of price volatility, or "beta." It is a mathematical measure assigned to the recent price volatility of a stock or an ETF (based on the stocks that compose it) and is one of the best indicators of risk. The beta is an indication of how volatile the stock or ETF is relative to the entire market. By definition, a beta of 1.0 represents the volatility of the stock market as a whole. Therefore, a beta of less than 1.0 means a security is less volatile and a beta of over 1.0 implies more volatility, and therefore a riskier security. The further away from 1.0 the beta gets under and over, the less and more volatile that stock is compared with the overall market. Stocks and ETFs with a beta of greater than 1.0 will tend to outperform the broad market when the market is going up and will incur greater losses when the broader market is going down. Stocks and ETFs with a beta of less than 1.0 will tend to underperform the broad market when the market is going up and will decline less when the broader market is going down.

The beta for the PowerShares QQQ is currently 1.2, which means that it is 20% more volatile than the overall stock market. In an up market, therefore, the QQQQ could be expected to rise over 20% more than the market in general, and in a down market it would decline by over 20% more. By comparison, the current beta for Bed, Bath & Beyond is 1.01, which means it could be expected to perform almost exactly as the broad market in general during either a rising or declining market environment. Finally, Apple has a beta of 1.7, making its stock price 70% more volatile, both up and down, than the market in general, and more volatile than the QQQQ.

The beta for a stock or ETF changes over time as market internals change. There are individual stocks that have a beta of less than .25 (e.g., some food stocks), while the beta of others can be well over 3.0 (e.g., some tech stocks). Again, this represents the price volatility of these stocks and measures the degree of risk of loss as well as the opportunity for gain when compared with the market in general.

There is a direct correlation between a security's beta and the price of its put and call options...the higher the beta, the higher the price of its options, and therefore the greater the amount of put and call writing income and the greater the potential return on investment from your "combinations" worksheet calculation. The natural corollary to this, however, is that the higher the beta, the greater the risk to you in your combination writing program. This is where your own risk tolerance and ability to sleep at night comes into play. To reduce the risk of large loss when writing combinations, high beta stocks *must* be avoided.

Second Question: What should the price differential be between the strike prices and the market prices of the underlying securities for combination writing?

On the relative scale of investment opportunities, writing uncovered put and call combinations is on the high end of the risk spectrum, although we can do much to manage this risk. As was stated earlier, the closer the market price to the strike price the larger the premium and the greater the *potential* return.   Thus, if maximizing the potential return was the only consideration, we might, out of greed, routinely write at-the-money calls and puts. Writing one month puts and calls, using a $36 strike price for both on the QQQQ with a market price per share of $36.09, as on the following page, is a good example.

Who would argue with an opportunity to earn $1,950 of premium income on a $11,917 margin requirement. That is a return of over 16% in one month, and a 186.64% annualized return. The rub is that this return is only "potential." It is true that if you wrote these puts and calls your broker would deposit $1,950 into your brokerage account the next day, less commissions. But to keep all of that, the QQQQ would have to be valued at exactly $36 on the expiration date 32 days later...wishful thinking at best. Any price above or below that on expiration would likely trigger an exercise of the option (puts if below, calls if above). Your return would be reduced by the amount of the difference between $36 and the price at expiration, times the number of contracts times 100 shares per contract (e.g., a $1,000 reduction in profit for each $1 of variance from $36. Therefore, an expiration closing price of $2 either above or below the $36 strike price ($34 or $38) would result in a small loss on the combination transaction. With any close lower than $34 or higher than $38 it would only get worse.

DATE: 19-Apr

CALLS

										%
x	x	x	x	x	x	x				
SEC. SYMBOL	OPTION SYMBOL	EXPIR. DATE	# OF CONT.	SECURITY PRICE	STRIKE PRICE	PREM.	MARGIN REQ.	# OF DAYS	PREM. INCOME	ANNUAL RETURN
QQQQ	QQQEJ	21-May	10	$36.09	$36.00	$1.00	$11,917	32	$1,000	95.71%

PUTS

										%
x	x	x	x	x	x	x				
SEC. SYMBOL	OPTION SYMBOL	EXPIR. DATE	# OF CONT.	SECURITY PRICE	STRIKE PRICE	PREM.	MARGIN REQ.	# OF DAYS	PREM. INCOME	ANNUAL RETURN
QQQQ	QQQQJ	21-May	10	$36.09	$36.00	$0.95	$11,687	32	$950	92.72%

ADDITIONAL FIRST CONTRACT MARGIN --> $0

TOTAL MARGIN NEEDED TO SUPPORT THIS COMBINATION TRANSACTION --------> $11,917
COMBINED % ANNUAL RETURN ---> 186.64%
COMBINED TRANSACTION INCOME --> $1,950

And, of course, the price on the expiration date is not the only thing we have to worry about. What if the market price of the QQQQ quickly dips to $32 or quickly rises to $40? The erosion of the time value of the premiums has not yet had an opportunity to occur, so we are faced with the prospect of an immediate sizeable loss. While you would have $1.95 per share of downside protection, you have no range between this put and call strike price in which to safely operate. If you are ever tempted to write a combination on any underlying security such as the one shown in this example where the strike prices are about the same as the current market price, do it on paper rather than for real for a month or two and then see how you feel about it...and consider only using ETFs.

Perhaps by now you may have concluded that a good strategy would be to write options with a lower put strike price and a higher call strike price in relation to the market price to provide a corridor of opportunity...a "comfort zone" so to speak. It is true that you will give up much of the return potential, but the sleep factor should improve considerably and you will still have the opportunity for an enormous return by any standard of measurement as seen on the next page. We will keep the expiration date the same, but write calls at a $38 strike price and puts at a $33 strike price, providing a $5 comfort zone in which to operate to achieve our maximum profit objective. Our premium income is reduced to $450 and our margin requirement is reduced to $10,000, with an opportunity to earn a 51.33% annualized return. With a total premium per share of $.45 received, the price of the QQQQ would have to be under $32.55 or over $38.45 on the expiration date before a loss would be incurred.

				DATE:	19-Apr					

CALLS

SEC. SYMBOL	OPTION SYMBOL	EXPIR. DATE	# OF CONT.	SECURITY PRICE	STRIKE PRICE	PREM.	MARGIN REQ.	# OF DAYS	PREM. INCOME	% ANNUAL RETURN
QQQQ	QQQEL	21-May	10	$36.09	$38.00	$0.25	$10,000	32	$250	28.52%

PUTS

SEC. SYMBOL	OPTION SYMBOL	EXPIR. DATE	# OF CONT.	SECURITY PRICE	STRIKE PRICE	PREM.	MARGIN REQ.	# OF DAYS	PREM. INCOME	% ANNUAL RETURN
QQQQ	QAVOG	21-May	10	$36.09	$33.00	$0.20	$10,000	32	$200	22.81%

ADDITIONAL FIRST CONTRACT MARGIN --------------------------> $0

TOTAL MARGIN NEEDED TO SUPPORT THIS COMBINATION TRANSACTION --------> $10,000
COMBINED % ANNUAL RETURN ------------------------------------> 51.33%
COMBINED TRANSACTION INCOME ------------------------------> $450

Does making this change assure that no loss will be experienced? No. But clearly it improves the odds for success. A loss would be incurred only if the stock price fell by more than 10% in one month (120% annualized) or rose by more than 6.5% in one month (78% annualized). It provides the comfort zone during the month before the expiration date, so if the price fluctuates either up or down there is room for it to move and remain a successful outcome.

Third Question: Which put and call option expiration dates will serve us best in our combination writing?

The best way to answer this question is to use the "combinations" template to calculate several alternatives using different expiration dates and also using different the strike prices. While our analysis has shown that there are some advantages for short-term as well as longer-term expiration dates, a program that incorporates combination writing using expiration dates principally in the one to two month range will likely provide the best opportunity for success. First, as seen by the previous graphs depicting the rate of decay for options, much of the premium is captured by the faster rate of decay that occurs in close to expiration. Second, if you are writing options with expirations in excess of two months, there is just too much time for prices differences in either direction to occur in the underlying stock that would take you out of your comfort zone. This may be acceptable for the put side of the transaction if you are very comfortable with the stock and are prepared to own it at the put strike price. However, on the call side of the transaction you have no alternative but to buy back the call at a loss or sell the shares short at a loss should there be a significant upward move in the stock prior to or at the expiration date.

After looking at various alternatives using the worksheet, if you feel that a longer expiration date is still advisable, you should consider the possibility of widening the comfort zone by using a lower put strike price and a higher call price. This should even be considered when going from a one-month combination to a two-month combination. You have previously seen the results of a one-month calculation using a $38 call strike price and a $33 put price. Let's look at the same strike prices now with a June expiration.

DATE: 19-Apr

CALLS

SEC. SYMBOL	OPTION SYMBOL	EXPIR. DATE	# OF CONT.	SECURITY PRICE	STRIKE PRICE	PREM.	MARGIN REQ.	# OF DAYS	PREM. INCOME	% ANNUAL RETURN
X	X	X	X	X	X	X				
QQQQ	QQQFL	18-Jun	10	$36.09	$38.00	$0.60	$10,000	60	$600	36.50%

PUTS

SEC. SYMBOL	OPTION SYMBOL	EXPIR. DATE	# OF CONT.	SECURITY PRICE	STRIKE PRICE	PREM.	MARGIN REQ.	# OF DAYS	PREM. INCOME	% ANNUAL RETURN
X	X	X	X	X	X	X				
QQQQ	QAVRG	18-Jun	10	$36.09	$33.00	$0.45	$10,000	60	$450	27.38%

ADDITIONAL FIRST CONTRACT MARGIN --> $0

TOTAL MARGIN NEEDED TO SUPPORT THIS COMBINATION TRANSACTION --------> $10,000

COMBINED % ANNUAL RETURN --> 63.88%

COMBINED TRANSACTION INCOME --> $1,050

The premium income is increased to $1,050 and the annualized return is actually greater than for the one month options (63.88%). The only problem with this is that you still have the same $5 strike price range, but two months for the stock price to move prior to expiration.

Now let's take a look at the June expiration, but using a $1 lower strike price for the puts ($32) and a $1 higher strike price for the calls ($39), as shown below. The premium income is reduced to $650 and the annualized return is cut to 39.54%, still a highly acceptable return for an investor.

DATE:	19-Apr									

CALLS

x	x	x	x	x	x	x				%
SEC. SYMBOL	OPTION SYMBOL	EXPIR. DATE	# OF CONT.	SECURITY PRICE	STRIKE PRICE	PREM.	MARGIN REQ.	# OF DAYS	PREM. INCOME	ANNUAL RETURN
QQQQ	QQQFM	18-Jun	10	$36.09	$39.00	$0.35	$10,000	60	$350	21.29%

PUTS

x	x	x	x	x	x	x				%
SEC. SYMBOL	OPTION SYMBOL	EXPIR. DATE	# OF CONT.	SECURITY PRICE	STRIKE PRICE	PREM.	MARGIN REQ.	# OF DAYS	PREM. INCOME	ANNUAL RETURN
QQQQ	QAVRF	18-Jun	10	$36.09	$32.00	$0.30	$10,000	60	$300	18.25%

ADDITIONAL FIRST CONTRACT MARGIN --> $0

TOTAL MARGIN NEEDED TO SUPPORT THIS COMBINATION TRANSACTION --------> $10,000

COMBINED % ANNUAL RETURN ---> 39.54%

COMBINED TRANSACTION INCOME --> $650

The importance of looking at a number of alternatives, particularly until you gain experience in writing uncovered combinations, cannot be overemphasized. Usually when you print out several different strike price and expiration date alternatives for the same underlying security, one will jump out at you as being the best fit. Trust your instincts on this, and if you are concerned about proceeding, do a dry run on paper for a period of time until you gain the confidence you need.

Fourth Question: At what point should action be taken if the market price of the underlying security moves toward, or past, the put or the call strike price and losses begin to occur?

Once the combination writing selection decision has been made and the transactions have been executed, what follows is a waiting game to see what happens. Hopefully you wait until the expiration date and nothing happens. Time is the option writer's best friend. Every day that passes with the market price of the underlying security remaining within the put and call strike range is a step closer to success. Option writing is a strategy that can provide you with solid investment returns if little or nothing happens.

If the market price of the underlying security begins a significant move in either direction, the writer needs to have a plan of action established in advance that will be followed to avoid significant losses. We will not suggest a single strategy for this contingency, but will rather propose several different strategies from which to choose, and you may decide to develop a modification of your own. As with many other aspects of this combination writing program, the choice should reflect the investor's own personal risk tolerance. Most important is that you do have a plan with which you are comfortable. While there are many ways to succeed as an investor, those with consistent results are usually the investors who have a plan and stick to it.

At this point we need to segregate combination writers into two camps. The strategy and plan of action will differ, depending on which camp you belong to.

PURE OPTION WRITER VS. OPTION WRITER/SECURITY ACQUIRER

Two different camps are necessary, because some investors may be willing to buy the underlying shares if the market price falls below the put strike price at expiration. Other investors do not want to purchase the underlying stock and regard the put side of the transaction in the same way as the call side of the transaction...a pure option play to earn premium income and not as an opportunity to acquire stock at a discounted price. Again, for purposes of the call writing component, it is assumed that you do not want to be in a position where you would have to short shares if the call were exercised.

Managing Losses:
The Pure Option Combination Writer

Clearly if the market price moves toward either strike price, you are likely to become increasingly concerned. First, your margin requirement *may* increase (you can always use your template to compute it at any time). You should also check with your brokerage firm frequently (especially if you do online trading, as it is very easy to check) to observe the changes in your margin requirement on their records. The broker will, of course, always notify you if you have insufficient margin, online and in writing. One thing should be very clear, regardless of your penchant for risk. You should never simply watch a stock price go against you well beyond your strike price and take no action under the hope that the price will snap back within your strike price comfort range. That's not to say that it can't happen that way, but it is not something you want to bet on, as the risk of additional significant loss is great.

We advocate that each investor adopt a specific option buyback regimen that would apply to all uncovered put and call writing transactions. Let's look at several suggested alternatives. We will assume that you have written the combination on the next page for purposes of explaining when you would close out your option positions for each of the following alternatives.

Alternative #1:
Liquidation at Strike Price

Description: If the market price of the underlying security reaches either the put strike price or the call strike price, buy-to-close both the put and the call position.

Action: Close both positions if the underlying security falls to $33 or rises to $38. This action is the most conservative of the proposed alternatives.

Alternative #2:
Liquidation at Strike Price + Put or Call Premium

Description: If the market price of the underlying security falls below the put strike price by an amount equal to or more than the put premium you received, buy-to-close both the put position and the call position. If the market price of the underlying security rises above the call strike price by an amount equal to or more than the call premium you received, buy-to-close both the put position and the call position.

Action: Close both positions if the underlying security falls to $32.55 or rises to $38.60.

| | | DATE: | 19-Apr | | | | | | | |

CALLS

x	x	x	x	x	x	x				%
SEC. SYMBOL	OPTION SYMBOL	EXPIR. DATE	# OF CONT.	SECURITY PRICE	STRIKE PRICE	PREM.	MARGIN REQ.	# OF DAYS	PREM. INCOME	ANNUAL RETURN
QQQQ	QQQFL	18-Jun	10	$36.09	$38.00	$0.60	$10,000	60	$600	36.50%

PUTS

x	x	x	x	x	x	x				%
SEC. SYMBOL	OPTION SYMBOL	EXPIR. DATE	# OF CONT.	SECURITY PRICE	STRIKE PRICE	PREM.	MARGIN REQ.	# OF DAYS	PREM. INCOME	ANNUAL RETURN
QQQQ	QAVRG	18-Jun	10	$36.09	$33.00	$0.45	$10,000	60	$450	27.38%

ADDITIONAL FIRST CONTRACT MARGIN ---> $0

TOTAL MARGIN NEEDED TO SUPPORT THIS COMBINATION TRANSACTION ---------> $10,000
COMBINED % ANNUAL RETURN --> 63.88%
COMBINED TRANSACTION INCOME --> $1,050

Alternative #3:
Liquidation at Strike Price + Combined Premiums

Description: If the market price of the underlying security falls below the put strike price or rises above the call strike price by an amount equal to or more than the combined put and call premiums you received, buy-to-close both the put position and the call position.

Action: Close both positions if the underlying security falls to $31.95 or rises to $39.05.

Alternative #4:
Liquidation at Strike Price + Multiple Premiums

Description: This alternative would be essentially the same as Alternative #3, except if you have multiple combination writing positions, and all of them are performing well except one, the following would apply: If the market price of the underlying security falls below the put strike price or rises above the call strike price by an amount equal to or more than twice the combined put and call premiums you received, buy-to-close both the put position and the call position.

Action: Close both positions if the underlying security falls to $30.90 or rises to $40.10. This action is the most aggressive of the proposed alternatives.

It is recommended that you close out both your put and call positions in all of the above situations for the following reason. The position that you are *not* having a problem with will be profitable by itself and the premium will have likely sunk to only a small fraction of the premium amount that you received. To continue to hold this position open with only a small amount of profit opportunity left would not be a good use of your margin resources (a possible exception would be if there were only a day or two left until expiration). You are better off liquidating both the put and the call position and writing a new combination to make the most of your margin.

As we discussed in Chapter 3, when the price of an underlying security rises, the price of a call option premium rises along with it, subject to the time value decay that occurs as the expiration date approaches. Similarly, when the price of the underlying security falls, the price of a put option rises, again subject to the amount of time value decay that may have occurred since the option contract was written. This means that under any of the above four alternatives you are likely to experience a loss, but one that should be manageable compared to what could happen if you didn't have a disciplined approach to closing out your positions in such a situation. The specific amount of loss will in part depend on how soon the price movement of the underlying stock occurs after your combination positions are initiated. The sooner the occurrence, the greater the loss, since there has been little or no time for the time value of the premiums to decay. The amount of your loss will also depend on how quickly you act after the price of the underlying stock reaches your action target price. You can see that it is necessary to regularly follow the price movements of the underlying securities on which you are writing combinations. You should keep ongoing written notes on all of your writing positions detailing the prices at which action should be taken, depending on which of the four alternatives you select. There is also always the possibility that some exogenous event may occur that could drive the underlying share price well above or well below your strike prices before you have the opportunity to take action, particularly if you are writing combinations on individual securities. It is imperative that you act as quickly as possible at that point to minimize losses, although as a practical matter the horse is already out of the barn.

Clearly, regardless of which action alternative you pick, regardless of what the betas are for the underlying securities you select, regardless of which strike prices and expiration dates you select, *you will have losses* in some of your option writing combinations. This is to be expected. Our objective is that on an ongoing basis the collective amount of premiums you earn significantly outweighs the amount of premiums you buy back to close so that overall your return on investment achieves or exceeds your expectations. If that is not being reached over time, you would obviously be better off considering other investment alternatives.

Managing Losses:
The Option Combination Writer/ Security Acquirer

As we discussed previously, you should only write uncovered options on securities with which you are very comfortable and which you would be willing to own for the long-term. Many investors may not wish to actually own the securities, but at least they would not be wholly uncomfortable doing so if circumstances were to put the shares into their hands. Other investors may actually view the acquiring of the underlying shares when their put contracts are assigned as an opportunity. They have bought shares they like at a discount from what the share price was when the option combinations were written and earned premium income while they waited.

A different plan of action is needed for these investors. They will be concerned primarily if the price of the underlying shares increase, not decrease, as they are prepared to buy the shares if put to them. Let's first look at the consequences of a rising stock price.

If you are a combination writer/security acquirer, you will likely only become increasingly concerned if the market price advances toward the call strike price. First, your margin requirement *may* increase (again, you can always use your template to compute it at any time). You should check with your brokerage firm frequently (especially if you do online trading, as it is very easy to check) to observe the changes in your margin requirement on their records. The broker will, of course, always notify you if you have insufficient margin, online and in writing. Again, you should never simply watch a stock price go against you well beyond your call strike price and take no action under the hope that the price will snap back within your strike price comfort range. That's not to say that it can't happen that way, but it is not something you want to bet on, as the risk of additional significant loss is great.

We advocate that each investor adopt a specific option buyback regimen that would apply to all uncovered call writing transactions. And, as long as you are comfortable with owning the underlying security at the put strike, you will take no action on the put side of the transaction.

Let's look at several suggested alternatives for the same combination we discussed previously to explain when you would close out your call option position for each of the following alternatives.

Alternative #1:
Liquidation at Strike Price Liquidation

Description: If the market price of the underlying security reaches the call strike price, buy-to-close both the put and the call position.

Action: Close both positions if the underlying security rises to $38. If the market price falls below the put strike price, retain both uncovered option positions until the expiration date.

DATE: 19-Apr

CALLS

SEC. SYMBOL	OPTION SYMBOL	EXPIR. DATE	# OF CONT.	SECURITY PRICE	STRIKE PRICE	PREM.	MARGIN REQ.	# OF DAYS	PREM. INCOME	% ANNUAL RETURN
QQQQ	QQQFL	18-Jun	10	$36.09	$38.00	$0.60	$10,000	60	$600	36.50%

PUTS

SEC. SYMBOL	OPTION SYMBOL	EXPIR. DATE	# OF CONT.	SECURITY PRICE	STRIKE PRICE	PREM.	MARGIN REQ.	# OF DAYS	PREM. INCOME	% ANNUAL RETURN
QQQQ	QAVRG	18-Jun	10	$36.09	$33.00	$0.45	$10,000	60	$450	27.38%

ADDITIONAL FIRST CONTRACT MARGIN --> $0

TOTAL MARGIN NEEDED TO SUPPORT THIS COMBINATION TRANSACTION --------> $10,000

COMBINED % ANNUAL RETURN --> 63.88%

COMBINED TRANSACTION INCOME ---> $1,050

Alternative #2:

Liquidation at Strike Price + Call Premium

Description: If the market price of the underlying security rises above the call strike price by an amount equal to or more than the call premium you received, buy-to-close both the put position and the call position.

Action: Close both positions if the underlying security rises to $38.60. If the market price falls below the put strike price, retain both uncovered option positions until the expiration date.

Alternative #3:

Liquidation at Strike Price + Combined Premiums

Description: If the market price of the underlying security rises above the call strike price by an amount equal to or more than the combined put and call premiums you received, buy-to-close both the put position and the call position.

Action: Close both positions if the underlying security rises to $39.05. If the market price falls below the put strike price, retain both uncovered option positions until the expiration date.

Alternative #4:

Liquidation at Strike Price + Multiple Premiums

Description: This alternative would be essentially the same as Alternative #3, except if you have multiple combination writing positions, and all of them are performing well except one, the following would apply: If the market price of the underlying security rises above the call strike price by an amount equal to or more than twice the combined put and call premiums you received, buy-to-close both the put position and the call position.

Action: Close both positions if the underlying security rises to $40.10. If the market price falls below the put strike price, retain both uncovered option positions until the expiration date.

As stated earlier, if you close out your call position in any of the above situations, it is recommended that you close out your put position as well for the following reason. The put position will be profitable by itself and the premium will have likely sunk to only a small fraction of the premium amount that you received. To continue to hold this position open with only a small amount of profit opportunity left, even though you would be willing to purchase the underlying stock, would not be a good use of your margin resources (possible exception would be if there were only a day or two left until expiration). You are better off liquidating both the put and the call position and writing a new combination to make the most of your margin.

USING COVERED CALL WRITING ON ACQUIRED SHARES FROM ASSIGNED PUTS

For those investors who are interested in acquiring the underlying shares at the put strike price, their option contracts will be exercised and assigned if the market price is below the put strike price on the expiration date. If this occurs, it transforms the uncovered (short) put position into a long stock position. If the investor chooses to retain the shares, writing covered calls can be a very attractive complement to put writing. While the potential annualized returns are not nearly as great using covered call writing as with uncovered combination writing, the risk is far less. Covered call writing is the most conservative of all option strategies (more conservative than simply owning shares by themselves), yet there is an opportunity to earn double-digit returns employing a covered call writing strategy on shares that are owned.

It is beyond the scope of this book to discuss covered call writing in detail. Investors are referred to the following other books by this author that provide the education, implementation programs and software templates geared specifically to covered call writing. They are all available through Arrow Publications (www.arrowpublications.net) at a discount:

Covered Call Writing Demystified: Double-Digit Returns on Stocks in a Slower Growth Market for the Conservative Investor (ISBN 0-9715514-0-5) – for covered call writing on individual stocks

Covered Call Writing With Exchange Traded Funds: Double-Digit Returns, Diversification, Downside Protection (ISBN 0-9715514-2-1) – For covered call writing on Exchange Traded Funds.

Covered Call Writing With Qs and Diamonds: Double-Digit Returns on Ready-Made Portfolios (ISBN 0-9715514-3-X) – For covered call writing on two of the most liquid Exchange Traded Funds that are especially suitable for writing calls due to liquidity and dollar increment strike prices.

ROLLING DOWN THE CALL STRIKE PRICE

Whether you are a pure option writer or an option writer/security acquirer, a tactic you might be able to use on occasion is known as "rolling down. " Let's say you have implemented the same QQQQ put and call combination we have been discussing. Some time after you have executed the transactions, but before the expiration date, the price of the QQQQ declines to, say, $34. Due to the decline (and perhaps also to decay in time value, depending on how much time has elapsed), the call premium has come down substantially from the amount you received, so that most of your gain on the call has already been realized. If you were to buy back your $38 strike price call to close out this position, you would have a significant gain. You could then sell-to-open a new call position with the same expiration date but at a lower strike price, thereby increasing your opportunity for additional call premium income, but not disturbing the put position. For example, at a QQQQ price of $34, perhaps the original $.60 call premium is now trading at $.20. You would have realized 2/3 of gain if you bought back the calls at $.20, for a profit of $400. You could then write the same number of contracts at a lower call strike price, say $36, and receive a higher premium, perhaps $.45 or so, again depending on how close the expiration date is. If you did this, you would now have a revised comfort zone of $33 to $36, with the QQQQ price at $34. If the QQQQ price went back up, rolling down may have been a mistake. This is not something you will want to do often, but on occasion it might make sense and allow you to increase your overall call writing income.

ROLLING UP THE PUT STRIKE PRICE

Likewise, if you are a pure option writer, you may on occasion wish to consider the mirror image of rolling down by buying back your put position to close when the price of the underlying security rises and then "rolling up." (Note: for the option writer/security acquirer who wishes to purchase the underlying stock at the original put strike price, this does not apply.) Again, let's say you have implemented the same QQQQ put and call combination we have been discussing. Some time after you have executed the transactions, but before the expiration date, the price of the QQQQ rises to, say, $37 ½. Due to the rise (and perhaps also to decay in time value, depending on how much time has elapsed), the put premium has come down substantially from the amount you received, so that most of your gain on the put has already been realized. If you were to buy back your $33 strike price put to close out this position, you would have a significant gain. You could then sell-to-open a new put position with the same expiration date but at a higher strike price, thereby increasing your opportunity for additional put premium income, but not disturbing the call position. For example, at a QQQQ price of $37 ½, perhaps the original $.45 put premium is now trading at $.15. You would have realized 2/3 of gain if you bought back the puts at $.15, for a profit of $300. You could then write the same number of contracts at a higher put strike price, say $35, and receive a higher premium, perhaps $.35 or so, again depending on how close the expiration date is. If you did this, you would now have a revised comfort zone of $35 to $38, with the QQQQ price at $37 ½. If the QQQQ price went back down, rolling up may have been a mistake. As with rolling down, this is not something you will want to do often, but on occasion it might make sense and allow you to increase your overall put writing income if you are a pure put writer who has no interest in purchasing the underlying stock in your writing combinations.

Fifth Question: How many uncovered option combination contracts can I write before I become overextended?

Writing uncovered put and call option combinations allows the investor to potentially achieve solid double-digit and in cases triple-digit annualized returns, in part due to the substantial leverage available from the low initial margin requirement. The result is that it may be tempting for the investor to overextend himself by writing too many option contracts. If the prices of the underlying securities on which you are writing combinations move below the put strike prices or above the call strike prices, the result could be a significantly increased margin requirement. This proclivity of some investors to overextend themselves by writing too many contracts, thereby risking unmanageable losses, is one of the primary disadvantages of uncovered option writing.

From the standpoint of the broker's margin requirement, it may appear that writing a large number of put and call combination contracts can be supported by the assets in the brokerage account. It must be recognized, however, that a significant downward or upward move in the prices of several of the underlying stocks may necessitate adding additional cash or securities to the account to avoid being sold out by the broker at a loss if a margin call is not met in time. Due to this leverage, the investor must have discipline. There are some precautions that should be taken to make overextension less likely:

- If you utilize the put writing component of the combination as an opportunity to acquire stocks at a discount in addition to getting the put writing premium income, only write as many put contracts as you are fully prepared to purchase the shares they represent should all of the market prices go below the strike prices.

- Either keep sufficient cash and/or securities in your brokerage account, or have such additional resources in other accounts that could be added to your account, if you receive a margin call. Recognize that if you do not have access to sufficient resources to do this, you may be compelled at times by your broker to buy back your contracts at a loss if you cannot meet a margin call.

- Prior to trading, use the Excel® template "combinations" to model different assumptions on the number of put and call contracts and price changes in the underlying securities and option contracts to see what the margin requirements would be under those assumptions. Compare the results with the cash/securities you have in your brokerage account or otherwise available for adequacy.

Sometimes brokerage firms will take steps themselves to reduce the risk you are taking. They do this by assigning a higher margin requirement for certain underlying securities than for others. For example, under the second margin calculation method a broker might assign a 30% margin requirement for ETFs such as the Qs and Diamonds, 35% to most other stocks, and as much as 50% to 60% for riskier stocks with a very high beta. Assigning a greater margin requirement has the effect of reducing the number of option contracts you should write. Check with your brokerage firm or prospective brokerage firms to determine their policies and adjust the percentages in your calculations accordingly.

Since uncovered put and call option combination writing is inherently a high risk investment strategy, in part due to investor's ability to utilize high margin leverage, precautions should be taken wherever possible to mitigate that risk, including a conservative approach to the total number of put and call option contracts written relative to the investor's investment resources. Starting your combination writing program by writing fewer contracts until your knowledge and comfort level increases is infinitely wiser than beginning with larger commitments that may result in significant losses. "Walking" before "running" is a good practice. And an exit plan is also critically important.

A NIGHTMARE EXAMPLE

The following scenario actually occurred between October 18, 2004 and November 19, 2004. It clearly illustrates the critical importance of the two practices enumerated in Chapter 4 to mitigate risk when writing uncovered calls. All of these numbers are real.

After successfully completing its IPO on August 19, 2004 at an $85 share price, the price of Google shares (ticker symbol GOOG) staged a 74% rise to $148 by October 18. After such an increase, an investor could be forgiven for thinking that the shares might be due for a pause, if not some retracement of such significant gains. Yet with such a volatile stock, a writer of uncovered Google calls would still need a large comfort zone. In reviewing an option chain on October 18, an investor would have found a one-month call (expiration date November 19) at a strike price of $175 with a call premium of $1.35. Perhaps after a previous runup of $63 per share, a bet that it would not increase further by more than $27 ($175 - $148) over the next month might seem reasonable, even for such a high beta stock. A glance at the uncovered call portion of the template for a write of ten Google November $175 contracts would have appeared as indicated on the next page. All the share price would have to do is remain under $175 per share on November 19 for an investor to reap a quick gain of $1,350, an annualized yield of over 65% on the initial margin requirement of $23,550…or so it would seem.

										%
CO. SYM.	OPTION SYM.	EXPIR. DATE	# OF CONT.	SHARE PRICE	STRIKE PRICE	PREM.	MARGIN REQ.	# OF DAYS	PREM. INC.	ANNUAL YIELD
GOOG	GOUKO	19-Nov	10	$148.00	$175.00	$1.35	$23,550	32	$1,350	65.39%

DATE: 18-Oct — CALLS

Google was about to release its first earnings report after the IPO during this timeframe. Because the company had not given any guidance on what investors might expect, there was a broad range of estimates being suggested by analysts who followed the company. (Note: an investor who followed Practice #1(2) would not have written these options due to the possibility of significant positive news.) This earnings confusion caused the stock price to drop to about $140 on October 20, which would no doubt have given an investor some comfort that he had made the right decision by writing these uncovered calls. The next day after the market's close the company reported earnings that were well above the range of estimates. The result was that over the next nine trading days the share price advanced steadily to an intraday high of $201.60! The November $175 call contracts were in the money by $26.60.

Even if the investor had not followed Practice #1, diligently following Practice #2 would have gotten him out early enough to avoid catastrophic loss. Each uncovered option writer needs to establish an exit plan based on his own tolerance for pain. What would have happened if this investor had simply hung on until the stock price hit $200? This was the result:

DATE:	**3-Nov**									
CALLS										
x	x	x	x	x	x	x				
CO. SYM.	**OPTION SYM.**	**EXPIR. DATE**	**# OF CONT.**	**SHARE PRICE**	**STRIKE PRICE**	**PREM.**	**MARGIN REQ.**	**# OF DAYS**	**PREM. INC.**	**% ANNUAL YIELD**
GOOG	GOUKO	19-Nov	10	$200.00	$175.00	$27.00	$112,000	16	$27,000	549.94%

Note that the margin requirement has increased from $23,550 to $112,000. Unless the investor had significant additional cash or assets in his account, there would likely be a margin call with the possibility that the broker/dealer would liquidate this and/or other positions to meet the margin call. Far worse yet is the fact that the call premium reached $27 per contract when the stock price reached $200. If the investor had repurchased the contracts at this point (or if the broker/dealer had liquidated the positions then) the investor would have incurred a loss of $25,650 ($27,000 - $1,350). Such a catastrophic loss in sixteen days could wipe out months and months of steady gains.

Ironically, the price of Google shares went on to close at $169.40, well below the $175 strike price on the November 19 option expiration date. So in the end result the investor would have had a winning transaction, with the options expiring out-of-the-money. Clearly however no investor, regardless of the extent of his resources, would have been able to stand the pain of holding onto this position until the expiration date. This is particularly true, since some analysts as well as Jim Cramer on CNBC were suggesting that Google shares could advance to as high as $250.

This is an extreme example of how things can go wrong, although it is a real life example. It clearly depicts the high level of risk that an uncovered call writer could be taking under very adverse circumstances. The two practices would have totally avoided or significantly mitigated this risk. They demonstrate the importance of implementing them for any investor who plans to write uncovered calls or uncovered put and call combinations.

USING TECHNICAL ANALYSIS WITH WRITING PUT AND CALL COMBINATIONS

Using a consistent program such as the one we have outlined, double-digit returns from put and call combination writing is possible to achieve on a consistent basis without the use of either "fundamental analysis" or "technical analysis" by writing combinations on a well diversified group of individual securities or ETFs. The latter, in particular, would be the simplest possible world for the investor, involving no individual stock selection for an equity portfolio. An investor could simply follow these steps:

(1) write puts at the lowest strike price and calls at the highest strike price that will achieve the investment return objective using the desired expiration date;

(2) take no action as long as the price of the underlying securities remain within the put and call strike price range;

(3) buy back the options if the price moves beyond the strike prices according to the alternative the investor has chosen in Chapter 4.

Some investors would like to try to improve their success rate, and accordingly their investment return "batting average," by timing their put and call writing based on technical market considerations. The goal would simply be to answer the question: *What do I think is going to happen to the market price of the underlying security from the date I write options until they expire?* The answer to this question will determine which put and call strike prices you select and may also influence the expiration date you select...possibly even the underlying securities you select as well if you apply technical analysis to the broader market. Obviously this is seldom, if ever, an easy question to answer. Even "expert" portfolio managers, economists and stock traders, not to mention the "average" investor, have trouble arriving at a good answer to this question with any consistency.

But, if you could identify a likely upward or downward path for a stock on which you wish to write uncovered puts and calls, you might decide to write either the put or the call first and then follow up later with the other leg of the combination. While many combination writers have the practice of always writing both the put and the call at the same time, there is nothing that says you can't do the put now and the call later or vice versa. If, based on technical analysis, you were convinced that a stock was about to rise, you might well write the puts now and wait to write the calls later after a rise occurs. If technical indicators seem to agree that a stock may decline in price, writing calls now and puts later may work best. If this price action turned out to be correct, your returns and probability of success would be enhanced. Whether you initiate both sides of the combination at once or do it in stages would depend on the confidence you have in your ability to read the technical indicator tea leaves.

Evaluating technical indicators may benefit the investor on a short-term basis by applying the results to decisions about when to be in the market, when to be out of the market, when to write puts, when to write calls, the degree of spread between the strike prices and the market price of the underlying shares, and choice of expiration dates.

The value of technical analysis depends on whether you are able to use it in a way that makes you more money than if you did not take the time to use it...and it does take some time. Some investors regard it as smoke and mirrors while others rely on it exclusively for virtually all of the investment decisions they make. The purpose in presenting it here is to give the investor some additional tools to potentially enhance returns. You can decide whether or not it is worth the time and effort.

If you believed you knew what the direction of the market was going to be for the short-term future, you would probably want to make use of that information. Here are a few actions you might take if you could forecast the following events:

A significant market downturn
- sell shares you may own
- retain cash until a turnaround in the market is perceived
- write deep out-of-the-money puts to acquire shares at much lower prices, or avoid uncovered put writing altogether
- write calls that are closer to at-the-money
- write calls with longer expirations to provide greater premium income

A significant market upturn
- buy/hold shares

- write deep out-of-the money calls to allow for a large comfort zone, or avoid uncovered call writing altogether
- write puts that are closer to at-the-money
- write puts with longer expirations to provide greater premium income

A flat or slightly increasing/declining market
- follow the normal uncovered combination program as presented in this book
- if you write puts to acquire the underlying shares at a discount as well as for premium income, select put strike prices somewhere below the current market prices, depending on your personal preference and the price at which you would be willing to buy the underlying securities
- write uncovered puts and calls with out-of-the-money strike prices to create a comfort zone that will suit your risk appetite
- select expiration dates that will suit your personal preference

KEY SHORT-TERM TECHNICAL INDICATORS

Technical analysis has to do with the interrelationships between a group of elements relating to a security or the market as a whole, such as price level, price movement, volume of trading, and perhaps other factors. Essentially it deals only with perceived demand and supply issues relating to the security. Some investors use it exclusively in their decision making. Others use the "technical indicators" associated with this analysis along with fundamental analysis.

What follows are some of the more widely recognized tools market technicians often use to try to make predictions about market direction and individual security price direction. Use them as much or as little as you like, depending on your willingness to devote time to it and the results it produces for you. No representation is made as to their effectiveness.

TRENDS

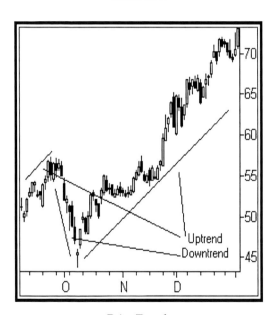

Price Trends

A trend reflects the direction of change in a stock's price over time. Trends exist in all time frames…minutes for day traders and years for long-term investors. For purposes of uncovered put and call writing, trends over a period of up to several months may be the most useful. Trends are classified as an "uptrend," a "downtrend" or "range-bound."

In an uptrend, a stock's price rises, often with intermediate periods of consolidation or movement against the trend. In doing so, it produces a series of higher highs and higher lows on the stock chart. In an uptrend, there will be a *positive* price change over time.

In a downtrend, a stock's price declines, often with intermediate periods of consolidation or movement against the trend. In doing so, it produces a series of lower highs and lower lows on the stock chart. In a downtrend, there will be a *negative* price change over time.

If the stock is range-bound, its price swings back and forth for long periods between readily seen upper and lower limits. There is no apparent direction to the price movement on the stock chart and there will be little to no price change over time.

A stock in an uptrend or downtrend will typically continue to rise or fall respectively until some change in conditions occurs. Stock chart readers try to locate the tops and bottoms, which are those points where a price rise or decline ends.

It is often said that "the trend is your friend." This bit of wisdom means that you will typically have more success in writing option positions that benefit by the direction of the prevailing trend than against it. Appropriate option decisions can be made using the trend to help determine the strike prices and expiration dates for the puts and calls you wish to write.

SUPPORT AND RESISTANCE LEVELS

"Support" and "resistance" deal with the supply and demand for stock. Too much available supply means more stock than investors want to purchase, so the stock price goes down. The opposite is true of demand. Demand for more shares than is available means upward pressure on the price of the stock. If the available supply and the current demand for shares are equal, then the price essentially moves sideways.

Support has to do with a declining share price, and a chart is necessary to determine support area prices. If a chart for a given stock shows that the price has declined to a certain level more than once--preferably several times--in the past where the decline halted and reversed, this would be considered a support area for the stock.

In other words, the supply of stock dried up relative to the demand for it. If the price has been above this support area and it declined down to it again, we might expect that this support area would hold and that the price would either remain at about that level for awhile or head up. So, if we were looking at a put strike price at which we would be willing to purchase shares, we might be more attracted to a strike price near a support area. If in the past the price had held several times at this level and then reversed upward significantly, it might be an excellent time to write puts, possibly selecting those that are somewhat out-of-the-money or conceivably even at-the-money for higher risk takers. If the shares decline to slightly in-the-money on the expiration date and the shares are assigned to you, you might benefit from an immediate technical upswing in the price. If a stock reaches a support area, it may not be a good time to be writing calls. None of this is to say that the price cannot just keep going downward. If it does, it simply means that the sellers won the battle over the buyers for the stock, and a new support level would have to be looked for in the chart.

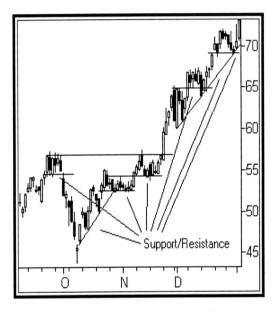

Support and Resistance Levels

Resistance, on the other hand, has to do with a rising share price. Again, a chart is necessary. If a chart for a given stock shows that the price has risen to a certain level more than once--preferably several times--in the past where the rise halted and reversed, this would be considered a resistance area for the stock. Here the supply of stock increased in relationship to the demand. If the price has been below this support area and it rose up to it again, we might expect that this resistance area would hold and that the price would either remain at that level for awhile or head down.

So, if we were looking at selling shares that we owned, we might be more attracted to take such action when they reached a resistance area. If in the past the price had held several times at this level and then reversed downward significantly, we might be inclined to either sell the stock if we owned it and avoid writing puts. This would be a good time to write uncovered calls. Of course, the price could just keep going upward. If it does, it simply means that the buyers won the battle over the sellers for the stock, and a new resistance level would have to be looked for in the chart.

We often see stocks trade within a price range, with both support and resistance levels being established. When the price eventually breaks out of that range, either on the upside or the downside, it may give us a signal as to which direction the stock will trend at that point.

VOLUME

Volume measures the degree of participation, or ownership, in a security. Stock charts display volume with bar type graphs known as "histograms," usually located at the bottom of the chart below the price graph. You can measure buying and selling interest by watching how many up or down days in a row occur and how volume on those days compares with days when the price moves in the opposite direction. The charts are often color coordinated. For example, a green bar may be used to indicate the volume for a day when the stock closes higher than the previous trading day, and a red bar may be used when the stock closes lower than the previous trading day.

Stocks that are bought with greater interest than they are being sold are said to be under "accumulation" (high volume on days when the stock is moving up). Stocks that are sold with greater interest than they are being bought are said to be under "distribution" (high volume on days when the stock is moving down). Accumulation and distribution often occur in advance of price movement. In other words, stocks under accumulation often will rise for some time after the buying begins (perhaps a good time to write puts). Alternatively, stocks under distribution will often fall some time after selling begins (perhaps a good time to write calls). Stock chart analysis works best on highly liquid securities, such as the QQQQ.

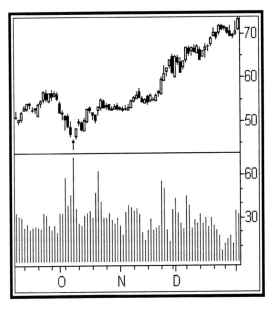

Volume

MOVING AVERAGES

A "moving average" shows the trend in the *average* price of a stock or market index over a specific period of time. As the name indicates, the time period "moves." For example, moving averages usually make use of a 10, 30, 50, 100, or 200 day calculation period, depending on the whims of the user.

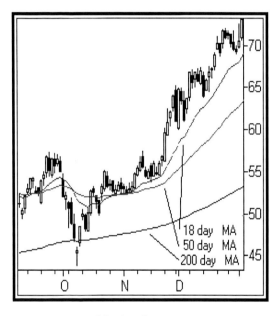

Moving Average

The longer the time period, the more the average gets smoothed out. And, when a new day is added, the last day drops off. So, if you were calculating a 50 day moving average for a stock, you would take the price--usually the closing price--at the end of each of these fifty consecutive trading days, add them all up, and divide by fifty. That would be the moving average for the first point on your chart. The next day you would add the closing price for that day and delete the first day's price, make the same calculation for the second point, and so on.

If the moving average line is moving in an upward direction and the current price of the stock crosses above the moving average, then a buy signal may be indicated (perhaps a good time to write puts). Conversely, if the moving average is moving in a downward direction and the current price crosses below the moving average, it may be generating a sell signal (perhaps a good time to write calls). Again, there is no assurance that either of these would be the case, so technicians usually give consideration to other indicators as well to strengthen their case.

A different twist on this would be a "weighted" moving average. This is calculated in the same way as what we just discussed, except that a higher weight is assigned to the most recent day and a progressively lesser weight to previous days. For example, if you were calculating a 10 day moving average, you would multiply the closing price on the first day by 1, the closing price on the second day by 2, and so on until you multiply the tenth day price by 10. You would add up all of these numbers and divide by the sum of the weights. This would give you a weighted moving average. In this case, a simple upward or downward turn in this average is believed to indicate a buy or sell signal for a stock, which would potentially be good put writing or call writing opportunities respectively.

THE VIX

The VIX can be viewed as a "fear and greed" index. It measures the implied volatility of S&P® 500 Index options and is therefore the best possible fit to measure expected volatility of SPY, the S&P® 500 ETF. The VIX is calculated and disseminated in real time by the Chicago Board options Exchange (CBOE). It is a weighted blend of prices for a range of options on the S&P® 500 Index. A high value means a more volatile market and correspondingly higher priced options, and conversely. It represents a measure of the market expectation for volatility over the next thirty days.

The following chart depicts a 10-day moving average of the VIX during a point in time. While the VIX over the years has ranged from a low of under 10 to a high in the 80s during the highly volatile market in late 2008, the long-term average for the VIX has been about 20. Extreme readings greater than 30 may constitute a buy signal (possibly a better time to write puts) and less than 20 a sell signal (perhaps a better time to write calls). Readings above 30 may indicate excessive bearishness, panic or an extremely high implied volatility (the up arrows). Readings below 20 may indicate excessive bullishness, complacency or low implied volatility (the down arrows).

The further the VIX increases, the more panic there is in the market. The further the VIX decreases, the more complacency there is in the market. As a measure of complacency and panic, the VIX is often used as a contrarian indicator. Prolonged and/or extremely low VIX readings indicate a high degree of complacency and are generally regarded at bearish. Some contrarians view readings below

20 as excessively bearish. Conversely, prolonged and/or extremely high VIX readings indicate a high degree of anxiety or even panic and are regarded at bullish. High VIX readings usually occur after an extended or sharp decline and sentiment is still quite bearish. Some contrarians view readings above 30 as bullish. The VIX Index can be found by requesting a quote and entering ".VIX" through many online brokerage accounts. It is also available on a daily basis by going to www.cboe.com and selecting "Market Data."

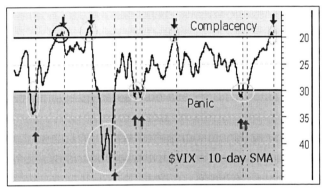

The VIX

THE PUT/CALL RATIO

Based on Chicago Board Options Exchange (CBOE) statistics, the Put/Call Ratio equals the total number of puts divided by the total number of calls. All stock and index options traded on the CBOE are included in the calculation.

Typically, there are more calls traded than puts and the ratio is usually below 1. When more puts are traded than calls, the ratio will exceed 1.

As an indicator, the Put/Call Ratio is used to measure market sentiment and is also regarded by many to be a contra indictor. When the ratio gets too low, it indicates that call volume is high relative to put volume and the sentiment may be overly bullish or complacent (perhaps a good time to write calls). When the ratio gets too high, it indicates that put volume is high relative to call volume and the market may be overly bearish or in panic (perhaps a good time to write puts). The ratio is often calculated as a moving average.

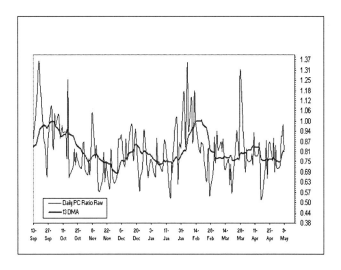

Put/Call Ratio

The Put/Call Ratio can be found on a daily basis by going to www.cboe.com and selecting "Market Data."

UPSIDE DOWNSIDE RATIO

The upside downside ratio is intended as a broad indicator of market direction in general. It takes the volume of the New York Stock Exchange stocks that are advancing and divides this by the volume of New York Stock Exchange stocks that are declining. A moving average of 10 to 20 days should be used.

A result above 4 is thought to be a positive buy signal (perhaps a good time to write puts) and a result below .75 is thought to be a negative sell signal (perhaps a good time to write calls). The chart shows an example of several buy signals (up arrows) and sell signals (down arrows) generated by this ratio.

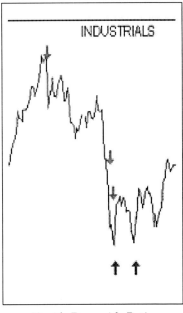

Upside Downside Ratio

BOLLINGER BANDS

Bollinger Bands are volatility based bands used to help identify situations where prices may be too high or too low on a relative basis. The base for the bands is a moving average and the band's width is determined by volatility.

When prices reach or rise above the upper band, they are thought to be too high (perhaps a good time to write calls). When prices reach or drop below the lower band, they are thought to be too low (perhaps a good time to write puts). Some technicians wait until the price has broken a band and then reversed price direction before considering the move a signal. According to its founder, John Bollinger, Bollinger Bands can be used for about any financial instrument, including individual stocks and ETFs.

Bollinger Bands

There are many other tools for technical analysis too numerous to mention. Obviously it would be a full-time job for an investor to try to assemble the data from which these indicators are formed. Fortunately that is not necessary.

Most online brokers allow you to build custom charts of securities and to add many of these technical indicators to the charts. There is no additional charge for this service. StockCharts.com (www.stockcharts.com) provides this as a free service, in case you do not have an online brokerage account. Whether through an online broker or through StockCharts.com you can build a chart and incorporate one or more technical indicators of your choice into the charts to assist in analyzing the potential for short-term price directions. You can usually save the charts for future reference, updating any changes if desired. On the next page is what a chart might look like on the QQQQ that incorporates several different technical indicators within one chart. Of course, separate charts could be developed for each indicator to avoid confusion.

The charting features available for free on BigCharts.com (www.bigcharts.com) can also be very useful. There are many services that offer technical analysis through charting and commentary in greater detail for a fee, both over the Internet as well as published periodicals. Never before has there been this level of data available to the individual investor to assist in timing decisions.

Investors who use technical analysis usually take a number of indicators into consideration to see if most are pointing in the same direction. If there is no pattern developing, it might be best just to ignore them and go solely with fundamental analysis.

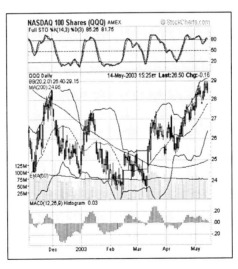

Multiple Technical Indicators

USING TECHNICAL INDICATORS
FOR PUT AND CALL WRITING DECISIONS

Technical indicators are typically used by investors to assist them in timing buy and sell decisions for stocks. While the indicators discussed in this chapter may be of use for that purpose, it is suggested that they also be considered for assisting you with decisions on (1) when to write puts and calls, (2) the strike prices selected and (3) expiration dates selected. Here is how these indicators may be useful in conjunction with the timing of your put and call writing to potentially increase your investment returns.

Technical indications:	Possible action to take:
Stock/ETF may have hit bottom and may be about to rise.	Write uncovered puts. Avoid writing uncovered calls until indicators stabilize or reverse.
Stock/ETF may have hit a top and may be about to decline.	Write uncovered calls. Avoid writing uncovered puts until indicators stabilize or reverse.
Stock/ETF outlook is neutral.	Write both uncovered calls and uncovered puts.

Most investors will never write in-the-money puts and calls out of personal discomfort with such an aggressive strategy, even if they have a good feel for technical turns in the market and for individual stocks and ETFs. Others may be willing to try anything and are prepared to take more risk to obtain greater returns. Taking more risk is not advocated, since even the most conservative put and call combination writing (deep out-of-the-money puts and calls on low beta stocks and ETFs) can provide double-digit returns. The broad spectrum of put and call combination writing is available to satisfy all needs. Success in using technical indicators over time may affect an investor's willingness to take additional risk.

BROKERAGE ACCOUNTS AND WRITING PUT AND CALL COMBINATIONS

Purchases and sales of individual stocks and ETFs as well as uncovered put and call writing transactions can be done through either a discount broker or a full-service broker. If you have an investment advisor or broker who is performing miracles for you, then he/she may be worth the extra money you pay in commissions. If that is not the case, it is very difficult to beat the low cost and ease of using an online discount broker. Although there are exceptions, most representatives of full-service brokerage firms are not trained to manage accounts for uncovered put and call combination writing.

You are encouraged to review some of the discount brokers listed in the Appendix of this book and compare commission costs for equity trades and option trades as well as compare services offered. If you become a serious combination writer, you will be incurring commissions from your writing activities on a regular basis. It is therefore important to keep your commission costs as low as possible in order to maximize the opportunity to realize your investment objective. This chapter operates under the assumption that you are trading through an online discount broker. While covered call writing can be done with all online brokers, some allow uncovered put and call writing transactions to be completed online while others offer it only to their "active traders" and large investors. Some brokers do not allow any online trading for uncovered option writing, so one of their representatives must be contacted by telephone. Depending on the volume of trades you do and the size of your account(s), you may or may not be able to initiate your uncovered option writing trades online. By phoning the brokers of your choice you should be able to determine whether uncovered writing is available to you online, and if not, what the procedures and commission schedule will be to conduct your trades. The author's view is that it is best to trade online if at all possible, and the following assumes that you are doing your uncovered put and call combination writing in that manner.

ONLINE DISCOUNT BROKERS

With just a little experience you will find that trading uncovered options online is much quicker, easier and less expensive than dealing with humans. For example, it is very cumbersome to have to call a human broker to find out what option strike prices and expiration dates are offered for the underlying shares you are interested in so that you can make decisions on your option writing program. You also need to obtain bid and ask quotes. Finally you need to place your orders and get quick feedback on whether your orders are filled. All of this information is available through an online broker as fast as you can make your fingers move on a keyboard and mouse. You really will not have any need to work with an individual unless you have some kind of problem with your account.

You must do your option trading with the broker where you plan to hold shares on deposit that you may have put to you in the future from your put writing activities.

COMMISSIONS

Discount brokers generally charge far less than full-service brokers, but even among the discounters there is a great deal of difference. Most of all you want to be sure you are dealing with a substantial brokerage firm who will be around for at least as long as you are.

Typically discount brokers charge for option trades based upon two components. First, there is usually a flat fee per transaction. This is why it is more cost efficient when you trade a larger number of contracts, as this component does not change regardless of how many contracts are traded. Second, there is usually a fee per option contract as well. This component tends to make it more expensive on a relative basis to trade a large number of option contracts on a lower priced underlying security or one with a small premium.

These two components are added together and charged as one fee per trade. As an example, let's say there is a $12 flat fee for a limit order plus $1.50 per contract. If an investor sells 10 put or call contracts using a limit order the commission would be $27. The larger the number of contracts traded, the smaller the commission as a percentage of the premium collected.

You can see that the way this fee schedule is structured, the commission does not vary with the amount of the premium collected. Therefore a commission schedule with a flat fee and per contract charge is one factor that tends to favor longer-term options, as they will always have more premium income per contract than shorter-term options.

Commissions on option trades tend to be higher than the discount broker commissions charged for share purchases or sales, which often run between $7 and $30, depending on the broker. But in recent years, fees on option trades have come down significantly and usually represent only a very small percentage of the put and call option writing income you will be collecting.

There are many online brokers such as TD Ameritrade, Charles Schwab & Company, E-Trade, Fidelity Investments, Scottrade, and on and on. An investor should be able to go to the Web site of any of the online brokers and check out the fees for stock and option trades very easily. Or, a phone call could be made to get the same information. Sometimes brokers charge you more to acquire shares that have been put to you through an assignment of a put than they charge for a regular purchase transaction. It would be a good idea to check this out when you are researching brokers if you may be acquiring shares through assigned puts so there are no surprises.

The "combinations" template used to select option alternatives can be easily customized to include option fees charged by your broker in the return calculations. Just add the appropriate charges your broker assesses on the worksheet to the right of the calculations.

Brokerage firms will only allow personal accounts to write uncovered puts and calls. IRA accounts, whether traditional or Roth, as well as other employee benefit accounts over which you may exercise investment control, are eligible only for covered call writing and "cash covered" put writing, where sufficient cash is in the account to purchase the shares if the put contract is assigned.

There are two important things to focus on when working with your brokerage firm on writing uncovered options. The first is getting the information you need to complete the Excel® worksheet so you can make your decisions on which puts and calls to write. The second is the process required to execute the option transactions in your brokerage account. When you write puts and calls your broker will credit the cash to your brokerage account the next day. All of the mechanics occur automatically. Not only will the cash be put into your brokerage account the next business day, but with a cash management account they should automatically invest the cash in the money market fund you have selected for your account. That way your premium income is earning interest until you decide to withdraw it or to reinvest it in something else.

THE OPTION AGREEMENT

You must be approved for option writing for the uncovered put and call writing by your broker through an application process. You need to sign an "Option Agreement" for each personal account you have with your broker so that you can trade uncovered options. The forms may be available online through the broker's Web site. If not, you need to call or write them, tell them that you want to write uncovered puts and calls in your accounts, and ask them to send you the necessary paperwork. They will send the Option Agreement form to fill out and also a publication they are required to provide called *Characteristics and Risks of Standardized Options*. This is a very informative booklet that reviews options terminology and theory, tells about the different kinds of options, how they can be used and the relative risks. As previously mentioned, some option strategies, such as writing uncovered put and call combinations, involve high risk and some, like covered call writing, can be very conservative. This booklet reviews it all. It is also available online at the Chicago Board Options Exchange Web site (www.cboe.com).

The purpose of the agreement is to help the broker assure that the investor has adequate knowledge about investing in options, has the appropriate financial wherewithal, and that the option transactions are suitable for the investor. You should go ahead and request the Option Agreement now to get the account set up so you are ready for this level of option trading.

The Option Agreement covers a wide variety of option strategies, so when you complete the paperwork you should indicate that you want to write uncovered put and call options (this will also automatically qualify you for covered call writing). You will also be asked about your investment knowledge and activity as well as your financial situation.

Finally, you will be asked about your investment objectives on the agreement. You should answer that your objective is speculation and production of income, which is consistent with uncovered writing of puts and calls.

Return the Option Agreement to your broker. It should be approved in a few days for trading if your broker believes you have adequate experience with options and the financial ability to support this type of option trading activity.

COMPLETING THE EXCEL® WORKSHEET DATA AND PREPARING TO TRADE

As previously discussed, you need to enter data in all of the columns on the Excel® worksheet that have an "x" at the top. This information should all be readily available from your broker. The columns are ordered for readability after the worksheet is complete, so you will not necessarily enter the data in the order of the columns. If you look at the bottom of the worksheet you will see a tab named "Expiration Dates." When you click on this you will see monthly option expiration dates going out many years into the future. You should select the dates you want, one at a time, by placing your cursor over the first date, clicking on the "Copy" button, then clicking on the "Put & Call Writing Combinations" tab, then placing the cursor in the appropriate cell under the "Expir. Date" column. Finally click on the "Paste" button and the date will be entered there. Next you need to type in the strike price you wish to review. If you have multiple expiration dates and strike prices you want to consider you should create a separate file for each using the worksheet and save them under different filenames that you will recognize.

You may not know the number of put and call contracts you wish to write at this point. After the other data has been entered and the calculation data (especially the margin requirement) has been reviewed, go back and enter or change the number of contracts.

Once you have this information in the worksheet, you are ready to begin looking up quotes. This may be done somewhat differently with various online brokers, but typically what you do is request a quote on the underlying security by typing in its ticker symbol. When you are getting an online quote, you should find the words "option chain" or "options" near the quote. By clicking on this, the brokerage firm's system should take you to a listing of all of the expiration dates and strike prices offered. Then scrolling up and down, you should be able to see the option ticker symbol for each option you wish to consider. On the next two pages are samples of part of a typical online option chain for puts and calls. These are for the QQQQ.

As you scroll down, note the ticker symbol for those you want and type in that information in the row under column B on the Excel® worksheet. Again, if it is not obvious after a little searching how to find the information you need, a call to the customer service center would be in order. As an alternative to obtaining quotations from an online broker, Yahoo! Finance, BigCharts.com, the Chicago Board Options Exchange Web site (www.cboe.com) and the CNBC Web site (www.cnbc.com) also provide extensive option chains for stocks and ETFs, however their information is not as current as you will find with an online broker who generally provides detailed real-time quotations.

After you have entered the put and call option symbols onto the worksheet, your row should be completed up to the premium column. Now you can get the premium quotes on the option symbols you wish to review and enter that information.

The option chain should give you a number of pieces of information about the quote you are looking for. Most importantly, it should give you the current bid and ask prices. These are even more important that the last price at which the option traded. It may have been some time since the last option trade, and the underlying shares may have gone up or down. This would mean that the bid and ask for the option have also gone up or down, sometimes causing the last trade price to be out of date.

QQQQ PUTS (STRIKE PRICES FROM $30 - $36)
MARKET PRICE OF QQQQ = $36.09

Puts								
Symbol	Date - Strike	Last	Chg	Bid	Ask	Vol	Open Int	Trade
-QAVQD	May 05 30.00	0.05	0.00	0.00	0.10	635	51,918	Trade
-QAVQE	May 05 31.00	0.10	0.00	0.05	0.10	1,656	3,327	Trade
-QAVQF	May 05 32.00	0.10	0.00	0.10	0.15	161	46,756	Trade
-QAVQG	May 05 33.00	0.20	0.00	0.15	0.25	848	28,090	Trade
-QAVQH	May 05 34.00	0.30	-0.05	0.30	0.35	18,922	129,811	Trade
-QQQQI	May 05 35.00	0.55	-0.05	0.55	0.60	34,141	227,014	Trade
-QQQQJ	May 05 36.00	0.90	0.00	0.90	0.95	29,274	139,040	Trade
-QAVRD	Jun 05 30.00	0.15	0.00	0.10	0.20	11	68,410	Trade
-QAVRE	Jun 05 31.00	0.25	0.00	0.20	0.25	20	40,193	Trade
-QAVRF	Jun 05 32.00	0.30	0.00	0.30	0.35	905	62,279	Trade
-QAVRG	Jun 05 33.00	0.50	+0.10	0.45	0.50	352	186,487	Trade
-QAVRH	Jun 05 34.00	0.70	+0.05	0.65	0.70	2,140	269,184	Trade
-QQQRI	Jun 05 35.00	0.95	0.00	0.90	1.00	11,325	314,203	Trade
-QQQRJ	Jun 05 36.00	1.35	0.00	1.30	1.40	6,999	119,526	Trade
-QAVUD	Sep 05 30.00	0.55	0.00	0.55	0.60	20	21,507	Trade
-QAVUE	Sep 05 31.00	0.75	0.00	0.70	0.80	0	80,228	Trade
-QAVUF	Sep 05 32.00	0.90	0.00	0.90	0.95	105	12,592	Trade
-QAVUG	Sep 05 33.00	1.15	+0.05	1.10	1.20	318	47,613	Trade
-QAVUH	Sep 05 34.00	1.45	+0.05	1.40	1.50	93	34,215	Trade
-QQQUI	Sep 05 35.00	1.85	+0.05	1.75	1.85	1,042	93,455	Trade
-QQQUJ	Sep 05 36.00	2.25	+0.05	2.15	2.25	2,301	74,451	Trade
-QAVXE	Dec 05 31.00	1.10	0.00	1.15	1.20	0	1,055	Trade
-QAVXF	Dec 05 32.00	1.40	0.00	1.40	1.45	0	696	Trade
-QAVXG	Dec 05 33.00	1.75	+0.05	1.70	1.75	15	2,594	Trade
-QAVXH	Dec 05 34.00	2.05	+0.10	2.00	2.05	70	1,544	Trade
-QQQXI	Dec 05 35.00	2.45	+0.10	2.35	2.45	330	10,327	Trade
-QQQXJ	Dec 05 36.00	2.85	+0.05	2.80	2.85	217	3,171	Trade

QQQQ CALLS (STRIKE PRICES FROM $36 - $42)
MARKET PRICE OF QQQQ = $36.09

Calls								
Symbol	Date - Strike	Last	Chg	Bid	Ask	Vol	Open Int	Trade
-QQQEJ	May 05 36.00	1.05	-0.05	1.00	1.05	28,827	101,058	Trade
-QQQEK	May 05 37.00	0.50	-0.15	0.50	0.55	21,241	235,350	Trade
-QQQEL	May 05 38.00	0.25	-0.10	0.25	0.30	24,525	158,682	Trade
-QQQEM	May 05 39.00	0.15	0.00	0.10	0.15	1,396	48,209	Trade
-QQQEN	May 05 40.00	0.05	-0.05	0.00	0.05	1,406	14,695	Trade
-QQQEO	May 05 41.00	0.05	0.00	0.00	0.05	30	10,594	Trade
-QQQEP	May 05 42.00	0.05	0.00	0.00	0.05	0	2,148	Trade
-QQQFJ	Jun 05 36.00	1.45	-0.10	1.45	1.50	3,887	73,229	Trade
-QQQFK	Jun 05 37.00	1.00	-0.05	0.95	1.00	3,088	94,884	Trade
-QQQFL	Jun 05 38.00	0.60	-0.05	0.60	0.65	36,812	111,754	Trade
-QQQFM	Jun 05 39.00	0.35	-0.05	0.30	0.40	1,182	71,817	Trade
-QQQFN	Jun 05 40.00	0.20	-0.05	0.15	0.20	505	34,383	Trade
-QQQFO	Jun 05 41.00	0.10	0.00	0.05	0.15	475	12,848	Trade
-QQQFP	Jun 05 42.00	0.10	+0.05	0.00	0.10	10	3,832	Trade
-QQQIJ	Sep 05 36.00	2.45	-0.05	2.40	2.50	501	70,335	Trade
-QQQIK	Sep 05 37.00	1.95	-0.10	1.90	1.95	2,737	141,838	Trade
-QQQIL	Sep 05 38.00	1.45	-0.15	1.45	1.50	849	107,314	Trade
-QQQIM	Sep 05 39.00	1.15	-0.05	1.10	1.15	726	93,913	Trade
-QQQIN	Sep 05 40.00	0.80	-0.10	0.75	0.85	144	31,993	Trade
-QQQIO	Sep 05 41.00	0.55	-0.05	0.55	0.60	30	9,520	Trade
-QQQLJ	Dec 05 36.00	3.20	-0.10	3.10	3.20	168	6,734	Trade
-QQQLK	Dec 05 37.00	2.60	-0.25	2.60	2.65	69	5,162	Trade
-QQQLL	Dec 05 38.00	2.20	-0.15	2.10	2.20	1,986	2,858	Trade
-QQQLM	Dec 05 39.00	1.80	0.00	1.75	1.80	50	1,631	Trade
-QQQLN	Dec 05 40.00	1.50	-0.05	1.40	1.45	40	6,284	Trade
-QQQLO	Dec 05 41.00	1.05	-0.10	1.10	1.15	30	1,046	Trade

After entering the option price (which should be at about the midpoint between the bid and ask, or perhaps slightly less), the rest of the data will be completed automatically. By entering the quotes in this way for each option symbol onto the worksheet, you are then in a position to review the worksheet and make a decision on which options you wish to write.

We will not review the decision making process again, as this was discussed in detail earlier. Of course your goal is to achieve your total return objective, basing your strike price and expiration date decisions on how you think the underlying shares will be performing between now and the time the option that you are considering will expire.

HOW MANY PUT AND CALL CONTRACTS?

One of the most important decisions you will make is the number of put and call option contracts you write on any given security. The reason this is so important is that the easiest way a combination writer can become overextended financially is by writing more contracts than can be supported by his financial wherewithal. The amount of cash or securities required by the broker to be on deposit is quite low in proportion to the number of puts and calls written. Therefore, should the price of the underlying security rise or decline, this leverage causes the margin requirement to increase. When examining put and call combination writing opportunities, the initial margin requirement may seem very manageable. As previously stated, however, it will change every trading day as the price of the underlying security and the put and call option contracts change. An upward movement in the underlying security will increase the margin requirement for the calls, while a declining stock price will increase the requirement for the puts. Should there be a major move upward or downward in the price of one or more of the underlying securities on which you are writing options, the margin you are required to maintain could rise significantly. Should the margin requirement rise beyond the level supported by the assets in your account, a margin call will be issued. This will require your *immediate* attention, as you are normally allowed only a short period of time (a few days or less) to either liquidate positions in your account or add additional cash or securities to support the higher margin requirement.

During the process of reviewing put and call combination writing opportunities using the Excel® worksheet, you should calculate different upward and downward price scenarios in the underlying security and the corresponding estimated price movements in the put and call contracts. This will allow you to determine whether you have adequate margin in your account or other assets available to support the number of contracts you are writing. If you would be at risk of a margin call under a significant price movement scenario that you think is a possibility, then you should reduce the number of contracts you are planning to write to make it more manageable.

ONLINE PUT AND CALL OPTION TRADING

After considering the alternatives, you have made a decision on a put and call option to write on a given underlying security. At this point you are now ready to use the online broker to execute the option transaction. When you are logged on to your brokerage account you need to go to the Web page that is used for option trades.

The information required by different brokers for their online system should be essentially the same. The pieces of it may just be located in different places on their Web pages. You will become familiar with your broker's pages very quickly after you do a few option trades.

When you have reached your broker's online option trading page, several choices should appear for the kind of option trade you wish to place. The buyer of an option would click on "buy" to purchase a put or call option or "sell" in order to close out his position. As you are not a buyer, but are a writer of uncovered call and put options, to initiate a new transaction you would click on "sell-to-open." You are selling...that is, writing...the option, and the transaction is an opening transaction. (Note: your broker may have a different name for this, such as "write uncovered put" and "write uncovered call." If there is any question about how you should execute your orders you should contact your broker). Enter the number of contracts, remembering that one option contract is for one hundred of the underlying shares in the U.S. You then need to type in the option symbol in the appropriate place to be sure you get the right contract (note: if you use an option chain you should be able to simply click on the option of your choice and the symbol is entered for you). Many online brokers use a minus sign, a period, or some other character either before or after the option symbol to differentiate quotes and trades for options. You will need to determine from your broker if there are any such special requirements.

There will also be a section that will ask you to click whether you wish a "market order" or a "limit order." A limit order requires that a "limit price" be set. If you select market order, the transaction will be carried out at the "best price available" when the order reaches the marketplace. It assures you that the transaction will be executed at some price. If there is only a $.05 spread between the bid and ask ($.10 for options trading at $3 or more), it should be safe to enter a market order rather than a limit order as long as the number of contracts offered for sale is at least as large as the number you wish to write. Information on number of contracts offered is sometimes available on the broker's online quotation system.

Sometimes the difference between the bid and ask for some option contracts can be wide and can work to an investor's disadvantage if a market order is placed. You could then end up getting your order filled for something less than the price you were expecting. For that reason, it is suggested that you generally *use limit orders and set a limit price* for your option trades. While you will not be guaranteed that your order will be filled, you will be assured that if it *is* filled the price you will receive will not be less than the limit price you have set...and it may be more, depending on the best price available at the time. Generally, when you are looking to do a trade on an option, you can expect to have your order filled at about the midpoint between the bid and ask, or perhaps a little bit closer toward the bid side. For very illiquid options, however, it may not be possible to realize more than the bid price.

You should click on "limit order" and then set a limit price you are willing to accept. For example, if the bid on your option transaction is $1.10 and the ask is $1.30, to have a reasonable assurance that your order will get filled, you should bid about $1.20. Or, you could plug $1.15 into your calculation worksheet, and if that amount would result in a return that is acceptable, you could consider entering your limit order for $1.15. For some option contracts there is sufficient liquidity that the spread between bid and ask will not be that wide (sometimes only pennies). For other more thinly traded options, the spread may be greater.

If you were to enter a limit price that is a bit higher than the midpoint between the bid and ask, it would probably take a rise in the price of the underlying shares, and correspondingly the call option, before your trade would be executed. The reverse would be true for put options. Since there is no assurance that the price would go up or down, your orders might not be filled.

There is a risk you do run, however, when setting a limit price. If by the time you get your order placed the price of the underlying shares has declined (for a call) or risen (for a put), then the option prices will have also declined and your orders will not be filled unless the prices of the shares return to where they were and the options rise again. The best guard against this is to be sure you have a very current quote on the bid and ask for the option contract and that you enter your limit order as quickly as possible after you have made your decision to write the option. In the event the share price changes, however, you should be prepared to cancel your option order and replace it with a lower limit price. Otherwise you would need to wait to see if the market price for your option recovers to your order price. You can see that much of this would be difficult if you were dealing with a live broker and had to be making phone calls back and forth until your trades were completed. Through an online broker, this is readily accomplished simply by pointing and clicking.

Of course, if the bid price fulfills your return objective and is acceptable to you, you could actually enter the bid amount as your price, but you should typically try to do at least somewhat better than that unless the spread between bid and ask is very small (e.g., 10 cents or less). You can plug in quotes for various premium alternatives into your worksheet to see what the returns look like compared with your objective.

There is another element that needs to be mentioned...an "all-or-none order." When initiating an option trade, all-or-none is a further restricting element of a limit order whereby you specify that either your entire order be executed at the same time or none of it is to be executed. For example, if you are trying to sell-to-open ten contracts, it is possible that only part of your order might be filled...say two contracts, with the order for the other eight not filled if the price of the option should quickly back off of your limit price. If you have to go in later and alter your price to fill the rest of your order, or if the balance of your limit order is not filled until a later date, your commission costs would go up. These trades would be treated as separate transactions for commission purposes.

The all-or-none order is a good idea if you are dealing with options that are thinly traded. It is not always possible to know how liquid the market is for the options you are trading, although some online brokers will indicate the number of contracts offered at the bid and ask prices. As you gain more experience with option trading you will get a feel for this. You should also be able to get volume information on option contracts from your broker's quotation system. At least initially you may wish to use all-or-none orders to avoid partial order fills. When you are initiating your transaction, either online, or through an automated voice response phone system, or with a live broker, you will be asked whether you wish to place any special conditions on the transaction. This will give you an opportunity to indicate if you wish the order to be all-or-none. There is one negative, however, associated with such orders. The broker may execute other orders ahead of yours at the same price that are not specified as all-or-none orders, so this may put you at a disadvantage when you are writing options on a security that is very thinly traded.

There is one final element to add. You also have an opportunity to indicate the time-in-force of the transaction. You can specify that the order will only be valid for the day, referred to as a "day order," or that it will be a "good-'til-canceled order," also referred to as "GTC." This would be entirely up to you. If you use orders that are valid only for the day and the order is not filled, that provides an opportunity to reevaluate what you want to do at that point. You can then enter a new order on the following day. With a good-'til-canceled order, the order will remain on the broker's books until it is filled or until you cancel it.

The process of trading options is essentially the same as trading stocks or ETFs. Since you are looking up quite a few quotes, computing a midpoint between bid and ask, and entering the information into the worksheet for review, it may seem more complicated at first. It is more work with options, but the end result can definitely justify it. And the more trades you do, the easier it will get. By the way, the more trades you do, the lower the commission rate you are charged by many brokers. When researching online brokers, be sure to review their commission schedules for higher volume "active traders" to see if you can qualify.

Once you have entered your order, you can check your online account at any time to see if the order is still pending or if it has been executed. Until it is filled, you will probably want to continue to monitor the price of the underlying shares and the option to see if you need to make any adjustment to your limit price if the market changes. Or you may wish to wait it out to see if the market price of the option recovers to your price.

In addition to receiving a brokerage statement periodically in the mail, you can, of course, also check at any time online to see a current statement of positions and cash balances as well as a transaction history. Some online accounts do not provide statements and confirmations by mail.

When you have written puts or calls, these options will show up online and on your brokerage statements as a negative balance until the options expire or are assigned. This is a "short position" offset to the cash you received into your account. It will reflect the current market price of the options as they fluctuate up and down based upon the price of the underlying shares. In addition to the price of the underlying shares, the other variable that will affect the price of the option is the time remaining until expiration. If the price of the underlying shares remains between your strike prices, the negative balances of the options on your brokerage statement will eventually diminish to zero as the time value decays on its journey to the expiration date.

INCOME TAXES AND WRITING PUT AND CALL COMBINATIONS

When you have success with a put and call option combination writing strategy in a taxable personal account it is going to mean more income taxes to pay. But, on the other hand, if things go according to plan you are going to have a lot more income than you otherwise would have had, so that obviously more than makes up for it.

As we have said earlier, when you write options you receive the premium income up-front into your account the next business day to use as you wish. The good news from a tax standpoint is that *even though you have the use of the premium income immediately, it is not taxed to you until the options expire* or until you close out your position if you buy-to-close, whichever occurs first. That can lead to some tax planning opportunities at times, depending on the time of year and the expiration date of the options you are writing.

DEFERRAL OF TAXES TO A LATER TAX YEAR

Let's say that you wrote put and call options on the QQQQ with a November expiration date and the options expired unexercised. Now you are ready to write another combination. You look at the premiums that are available for various expiration dates. You also look at your tax picture and realize that you have built up a lot of taxable income during this tax year and you would like to try to defer some income into the next tax year. What you could do is select put and call options with an expiration date in January or later of next year. By doing so, you have just deferred the income tax consequence into next year, even though the premium income is paid to you right now. You can do this on as many option contracts as you like. This can give you a powerful tax planning tool at times.

Speaking of tax consequences, perhaps the most important point is that the premium income you receive from writing puts and calls is "capital gain" for tax purposes. The bad news is that the premiums are almost always "short-term" capital gain regardless of the length of time the option was outstanding. That means your option writing income is usually taxed at the same rate as if it were "ordinary income."

You will need to report your option trades on Schedule D of Form 1040. Another template called "Schedule D" is provided to you with the "combinations" template. It will be discussed later in this chapter. If options you have written are either bought back or if they expire unexercised, you report the amount of gain or loss as a separate item on this schedule.

If you purchase the underlying shares at expiration as a result of an assignment of put contracts you have written, subtract the amount of premium income gain from the amount you pay for your stock. There is no immediate tax consequence to the put writer when the underlying shares are assigned. The put writing gain reduces the cost basis in the underlying security and is reflected in the overall gain or loss when those shares are eventually sold. If you hold the shares for over one year (current tax law) any gain or loss on the sale of the shares at the adjusted cost basis is "long term."

If you have written uncovered call contracts that are assigned at expiration, add the amount of the premium income gain to the strike price of the shares you short and deliver to fulfill your call contract obligation. There is no good reason for an uncovered call writer to allow call options to be exercised. You should always buy your call contracts back to close by the end of the last trading day before the expiration date if the calls are in-the-money. This will avoid the need for your broker to short the underlying security on the Monday following the expiration date (which may involve market risk, as the share price could increase further beyond the exercised strike price).

If you decide to close out your option position by buying back the options, any gain or loss would be short-term capital gain or loss in the year that the position was closed out. For example, let's say you wrote options in November that were not due to expire until the following year and you received $2,000 in premium income. In late December you bought back the options for $500. You would have a short-term capital gain of $1,500 for the tax year in which you bought back the options, not in the next tax year when the options would have otherwise expired.

Incidentally, although the premium income is taxable to you, option trades are not required to be reported by your broker to the Internal Revenue Service.

CAPITAL GAIN VS. CAPITAL APPRECIATION

Capital appreciation is different than "capital gain." Capital appreciation is an investment term that simply means an increase in value of a security, such as a stock, ETF or an option. For example, if an ETF goes from $28 to $35, it has experienced capital appreciation of $7 per share. Capital gain is a tax term that comes into play only when a capital asset, such as a stock, ETF or option, is sold. It occurs when the proceeds from the sale is greater than its cost.

You are likely aware that if you have capital gains you can offset them with capital losses to reduce your tax burden. So, if you had previously taken a "capital loss" on the sale of a security, you could use that loss to offset some of the gains you realize from your option writing income. If you have gains from writing options, you can also use prior year capital losses carried forward to offset the gains on the option income. And for any current "unrealized loss" in any shares you may own, you could sell those shares and then use the actual loss to offset option writing income.

ROLLING FORWARD

For potential share acquirers, our primary put writing strategy focuses on writing puts on shares of an underlying security that you would be interested in purchasing at a discount (the strike price you have selected). What can be done, however, if the market price declines below the strike price around expiration time and you decide you do not wish to have the shares put to you now? To liquidate your short put option, you could buy back the put to close out the position. You would likely incur a loss in this transaction, depending on how much the market price had fallen below the strike price (the amount of intrinsic value) and how much time was left until the expiration date. If the issue is simply one of timing (you would prefer to purchase the shares at the same strike price at a later date), after buying back your original put contracts you could write the same number of new put contracts at the same strike price but for an expiration date that is further out into the future. This is known as "rolling forward." If the new options have the same strike price as the old ones, the option premium received on the new puts will always be greater than your cost in buying back the old puts.

An example might help clarify this. Let's say you sold ten XYZ put contracts at a strike price of $55. Since then 2 ½ months have passed and the options expire about two weeks from now.

When you wrote the options you collected a premium of $2.50 for total premium income of $2,500. From the date you wrote the options 2 ½ months ago the price of the shares have gone from $60 to its current price of $52 per share. The put contracts you wrote are now priced at $3.50 reflecting the current intrinsic value of $3 per share (the $52 current market value less the $55 strike price) and the remaining time value of $.50 per share (the $3.50 current market less the $3 intrinsic value). Let's say you have decided that you do not want to purchase the shares on the expiration date, but would still be willing to buy them later at the strike price. You conclude that rolling forward is a strategy that makes sense for you. You get quotes from your broker on puts with the same strike price, but with a longer expiration date. There are several option expiration dates available to you. Which one you select is purely a matter of preference and planning. After review, you decide on the contract at the same strike price and with an expiration date in about 3 ½ months from now. Of course, it is always possible that the underlying share's price may rise above the $55 strike price by the new expiration date, in which case you would keep all of the new option premium income but would not be obligated to purchase the shares. The price of the option contract with the new expiration date is $5.50 (larger due to the longer expiration term). You are ready to roll forward.

First you buy back the old option contracts at $3.50 with an order to buy-to-close ten contracts. After the order is filled, you then sell-to-open ten contracts of the new option at $5.50. When that order is filled, you watch what happens until the new option expiration date approaches.

This sounds a lot more complicated than it really is. Let's first consider the sale and repurchase of the first option. You sold the initial puts for $2,500 and repurchased them for $3,500 for a loss of $1,000. This loss can be used to offset other capital gains you have earned. The new option transaction stands on its own. If held until expiration, the premium income of $5,500 would be taxed the same as other option transactions we have previously discussed. Of course, if the shares are put to you at the new options' expiration the cost basis of the shares you acquired would be reduced to $49 ½ to reflect the premium income you received from writing the second puts.

What you have accomplished is that you have bought additional time and thereby have extended out the time requirement of purchasing the shares at the option of the put holder. And, again, if the shares were to go back up above the strike price at expiration, you would not need to purchase the shares at all.

If the price of the shares just kept going down, there are a couple of choices you would have. First, you could just continue to roll forward the expiration dates by buying back the older contracts and writing new options as each expiration date approaches, just as we did in this example. The more the price declines, however, the more likely it becomes that the shares will eventually be put to you at the $55 strike price at some point. This strategy will not appeal to most put writers unless they are completely committed to buy the shares at the $55 strike price.

ROLLING DOWN

Going back to the example, another choice available would be to buy back the first put options and then write new puts with a lower strike price. This is referred to as "rolling down." Doing this can take the pressure off a bit, because if the strike price on the new option was $50, for example, you now have out-of-the-money puts that would not be exercised at expiration unless the shares continued to fall. If they did decline further, the shares would be put to you at $50, not $55, so you would have a lower acquisition cost for the shares.

Of course, the premium you would receive on a put with a $50 strike price would be quite a bit less than one with a $55 strike price. As you know, the lower the strike price for a put option, the lower the premium. Depending on how much lower the strike price is on the new option compared to the old option, and also how much further out the expiration is extended, the premium income on the new puts could be significantly reduced. You would have to consider all of the choices. The best alternative in some cases if you wish to defer purchase of the shares or reduce the likelihood of having to purchase them might be a combination of rolling forward and rolling down. A lot depends on your belief about the direction of the market. Unfortunately, of course, we cannot always accurately predict the future. And while using technical indicators may be of some assistance, there are no guarantees.

You can see why it is always best to write put options on shares that you are fully prepared to purchase at the strike price on the expiration date. You just let them be put to you and accept your purchase at the strike price rather than having to chase a falling share price by rolling forward and/or rolling down. Nonetheless, these are workable ways to defer the purchase of the underlying shares if the price of the shares falls below the option strike price. It is best to have a plan at the very start so that if the share price declines significantly you know in advance what action you will want to take.

Rolling forward can also be done with uncovered call contracts. We will not go through a detailed description of the transactions involved. It would be handled similarly to rolling forward put contracts. Instead of rolling down, as was just described for put contracts, rolling up can be done for call contracts. Again, this is done essentially the same as was described for put contracts, except you would be selecting a higher strike price for the new calls to remove the pressure as opposed to selecting a lower strike price for the new puts.

Rolling forward, rolling down and rolling up are described here primarily as devices to alter the tax consequences of option transactions under certain conditions. In general this is not likely to be a sound strategy for you, as there is always the risk that such action simply postpones the agony of loss to a later date. It is not necessarily a remedy if you are out of your comfort zone.

Incidentally, if you end up with a put and call that have different expiration dates, you still only apply one margin requirement to both positions…the one that is largest.

USING THE "SCHEDULE D" TEMPLATE

The "Schedule D" Excel® template can be used to prepare this schedule for your Form 1040 as you make trades during the tax year and as results are finalized on each expiration date on which you have option positions. This will spread out the recordkeeping during the year so that you don't have to prepare the entire schedule at tax time. Entering the data onto the worksheet should be helpful if you have a lot of options transactions during the tax year.

When you use the worksheet, you will note that there are numerous tabs at the bottom. The format is the same for each tab. This will allow you to prepare the schedule for many tax years without the need for separate Excel® files. Simply use the tab for the appropriate tax year.

	A	B	C	D	E	F	G
1	JOHN Q. TRADER		012-345-6789				
2							
3	SUPPLEMENT TO SCHEDULE D - 2009						
4	CAPITAL GAINS AND LOSSES						
5							
6		DATE	DATE	SALES			
7	DESCRIPTION	ACQ.	SOLD	PRICE	COST	LOSS	GAIN
8							
9	10 Bed, Bath & Beyond Jul $40 puts	19-May-09	20-Aug-09	$1,200	$0		$1,200
10	15 PowerShares QQQ 100 Jun $38 calls	19-May-09	5-Aug-09	$900	$150		$750
11							
12							
13	GAIN AND LOSS TOTALS			$2,100	$150	$0	$1,950
14							
15	NET GAIN						$1,950

First enter the name as it will appear on your tax return in cell reference A1. Then enter your Social Security number in cell C1. As transactions occur, you should start by entering the description in column A, beginning on row 9. A description of an option transaction might read as indicated here on rows 9 and 10. In column B enter the date you wrote the option contracts (enter as MM/DD/YY and it will be automatically formatted as shown). Enter the expiration date of the option contracts, or the date you bought back the contracts to close, whichever applies, in column C using the same format. Enter the net amount of premium income you received (after commissions and any other costs) in column D. Finally, enter your cost in column E. This will be $0 if the options expire and are not exercised. If you buy the option to close, this will be the net amount you pay after commissions and other costs. The amount of gain or loss will be automatically entered into the appropriate column and will be totaled at the bottom. If you need more rows for transactions, simply place your cursor on the number below the last row into which you entered data, click on "Insert" and then "Row."

At the end of the tax year, all you will need to do is to highlight the data you wish to print for your Schedule D supplement, then click on "File." When the drop-down menu appears next click on "Print Area" and finally click on "Set Print Area." You are now ready to print the schedule.

If you have a preparer do your return, simply give this supplement to your preparer. If you do your own return, on the Schedule D page in your tax package simply write or type "See attached supplement to Schedule D." Then enter the totals from the bottom of the columns of your supplement to your tax form Schedule D. Include the supplement after the Schedule D in your tax package when you mail it to IRS.

TRACKING YOUR RESULTS

You will note that on the "Schedule D" template there is additional data in columns J through W. This can be used for your own purposes if you wish to track your results and compare them with an objective you set. When you complete the data for a row in column D, the resulting loss or gain will appear in column F or G. Note the cell reference for this (e.g., G9). Go to the month in the same row as the month in column C, which is the date of expiration or the date you bought back the option and type an equal sign followed by the cell reference for the gain or loss. For example, for the gain of $1,200 in cell reference G9 shown in the sample schedule, you would go to cell reference J9 (the same row and under column J for January) and type =G9. This will enter the same data. Do this for each gain or loss in each appropriate month. The totals for that month will be automatically entered into the row labeled "Actual." If you wish to set an objective for each month, enter the amounts in the row labeled "Objective." The difference between "Actual" and "Objective" will then be automatically entered on the row labeled "Variance." The cumulative variance beginning with January and continuing to the end of the year will be automatically entered into the row labeled "Cumulative." This may be useful information for you to track how you are doing with your option combination writing program compared with your goals.

CONCLUSION

8

An investor's ability to write both uncovered puts and uncovered calls using the same margin presents a unique investment opportunity for those willing to assume higher risk as a tradeoff for higher returns. And clearly that risk is very high, given the inherent leverage that option writing entails. The fact that only one margin requirement is applied by the brokerage firm to the two uncovered transaction components of an option writing combination in effect doubles the already heady leverage that would apply to either leg of the transaction by itself. At the same time, if one leg of the transaction goes against you, the second premium from the other leg of the combination will provide some downside protection.

For the adroit, self-confident investor who spends a good deal of time watching the market and who has the discipline to follow a plan that will limit losses while offering the ability to generate double- and even triple-digit annualized investment returns, writing uncovered put and call combinations stands in a class by itself.

There are few investments where money can be made if nothing much happens. With combination writing, the investor has a double win in such an environment. While we will undoubtedly continue to experience volatility in the equity market at times, many of the best minds in the country believe that over perhaps decades to come we will witness a much different market than the past.

Warren Buffett, "The Oracle of Omaha," is one of them. In the past, Buffett rarely commented publicly about the market. However, just before the NASDAQ began its plunge of 77% in 1999 (as he shunned technology stocks, much to everyone's amazement), Buffett started to talk on occasion, primarily in *Fortune* magazine. At his annual meeting of Berkshire Hathaway on May 3, 2003, attended by 15,000 loyal believers, Maria Bartiromo from the CNBC stock market cable channel, caught up with him and asked him what he thought the future would bring for the stock market. His theme has been very consistent since his comment in 1999, as is exemplified by his response to Bartiromo:

> *If you own equities, over the next twenty or thirty years you'll get a reasonable return...maybe it's 6%, maybe it's 7%. People who expect 15% a year are doomed to disappointment.*

If 6% or 7% is all we can expect...before taxes and before inflation...we need to discover new opportunities to supplement or take the place of traditional investing. Investment strategies using options can present such an opportunity. While they are not new in terms of availability to us, they are clearly new in their use to almost all investors.

From the conservative perspective of writing covered calls to the high risk/ high reward potential of uncovered put and call combination writing, an opportunity exists to achieve superior investment performance that is actually enhanced by a stock market that is either growing or declining slowly. And if we can find an additional edge by using fundamental and technical analysis to help direct and time our option writing decisions, then we give ourselves an even greater possibility of success.

While few would disagree that uncovered put and call combination writing is high risk, there is a range of risk within that activity that constitutes conservative high risk vs. aggressive high risk. It is difficult to quantify the specific dollar risk in our examples. In loss situations, the amount of loss would depend on how soon the market price of the underlying security would make a significant move (vs. how much time had elapsed allowing decay of time value to take place), and the extent of that move. Also critical is how quickly the investor acts on his plan to close out the option positions, and whether rolling up, rolling down, or rolling forward is utilized. The program in this book is structured so that many more gains than losses should occur, resulting in the opportunity for double-digit annualized returns. No one need risk a dime to test these strategies sufficiently, as all of the information required to practice and measure results for any length of time is available today.

Only you can decide whether the lure of potential double- or even triple digit annualized returns is worth that risk, and how to manage that risk.

ALL-OR-NONE ORDER - A type of limit order which directs a broker to either fill the entire order or, if it cannot be filled, to fill none of it.

ASK - The price offered by an owner to sell a security, such as a stock, ETF or an option.

ASSIGNMENT - The requirement by the writer of an option to perform according to the terms of the contract by purchasing the underlying shares from the holder (buyer) of a put option or selling the underlying shares to the holder (buyer) of a call option. The option writer's broker handles the purchase.

AT-THE-MONEY - The strike price and the market price of the underlying shares are exactly equal or very close.

BETA - A mathematical measure of risk regarding rates of return on an equity portfolio, specific stock or ETF compared with risk and rates of return on the market as a whole.

BID - The price offered by a buyer to purchase a security, such as a stock, ETF or option.

BUY-TO-CLOSE – The placing of an order by an option writer to buy back the option in order to close out the position.

CALL – An option permitting the holder (buyer) to purchase a stock or ETF at a predetermined price until a certain date. For example, an investor may purchase a call option on AAA shares giving the investor the right to buy 100 shares (for each option contract) at $50 per share until September 15.

CALL OPTION WRITING (UNCOVERED) – An investment strategy for investors who are generally seeking to increase income by selling (writing) calls on individual stocks or ETFs. The option writer receives premium income in exchange for assuring that the buyer of the option can purchase the shares at the agreed price during the operative time period of the option contract.

CAPITAL GAIN – Occurs when the proceeds from a stock, ETF or an option sale is greater than its cost. When writing options, for example, if you receive $3 per share in premium income and the options expire worthless, your cost is $0 per share and the capital gain is $3 per share.

CAPITAL LOSS – Occurs when the proceeds from a stock, ETF or an option sale is less than its cost. When writing options, for example, if you receive $3 per share in premium income and you buy back the options at $4, the capital loss is $1 per share.

COMBINATION – For purposes of this book, the writing of both an uncovered put option and an uncovered call option at the same time on the same underlying security (also called a "strangle") in order to receive premium income from both writing transactions with only one margin requirement.

COVERED – Implies that the investor who writes a call option owns the underlying shares, so that if the stock or ETF is assigned the writer has the shares to deliver to the call holder (buyer).

COVERED CALL OPTION WRITING – An investment program for ETF owners and shareholders of individual companies who are generally seeking a conservative way to increase income from their shares by selling (writing) calls on the shares they own. There is also the opportunity for a defined amount of capital appreciation (for out-of-the-money calls) and the shareowner receives any dividends. The option writer receives premium income in exchange for assuring that the buyer of the option can purchase the shares at the agreed strike price during the operative time period of the option contract.

DAY ORDER – An order to buy or sell a security that will expire at the end of the day the order is placed if it is not executed.

EXCHANGE TRADED FUND (ETF) - ETFs represent shares of ownership in portfolios of common stocks which are designed to generally correspond to the price and return performance of their underlying portfolios of securities, either broad market, industry sectors, regions, investment styles, or international. ETFs give investors the opportunity to buy or sell an entire portfolio of stocks within a single security, as easily as buying or selling a share of stock. They offer a wide range of investment opportunities.

EXERCISE – In the case of put options, the holder (buyer) of the options requires the put seller (writer) to purchase the underlying shares at the strike price. In the case of call options, the holder (buyer) of the options requires the call seller (writer) to sell the underlying shares at the strike price.

EXPIRATION DATE – The last day an option holder (buyer) can exercise the rights in an option contract.

FUNDAMENTAL ANALYSIS – An attempt to determine the true value of a security based upon factors such as management quality, earnings, balance sheet statistics, and other elements of financial statements.

FUNGIBLE – Relates to assets that are identical and are interchangeable. For example, shares of the QQQQ (the NASDAQ-100 Index Tracking Stock) or the April $30 QQQQ puts are both fungible. All QQQQ shares are the same and are interchangeable and all of the QQQQ April $30 put contracts are the same and are interchangeable.

GOOD-'TIL-CANCELED ORDER (GTC) – An order to buy or sell a security that remains in force until it is executed or canceled.

HISTOGRAM – A bar chart representing a frequency distribution. The heights of the bars represent observed frequencies.

IN-THE-MONEY – Occurs when the strike price of a put option is above the market price of the underlying shares or when the strike price of a call option is below the market price. For example, the put option for a security with a strike price of $50 when the security is trading at $48 would be $2 in-the-money.

INTRINSIC VALUE – That part of an option's market price which is in-the-money. For example, if the current market price of an option is $3 ½ and the option is in-the-money by $2, the intrinsic value is $2 and the time value is $1 ½. If an option is at-the-money or out-of-the-money there is no intrinsic value.

LEAPS – An acronym for Long-Term Equity Anticipation Securities. These are options with expiration dates extending up to three years, which is well beyond the term of regular options.

LEVERAGE – An attempt by an investor to increase the rate of return from an investment by assuming additional risk. Examples of leverage would be buying securities on margin, using low margin requirements to write put and call combination contracts and speculating by purchasing options.

LIMIT ORDER – An order to execute a transaction only at a specified limit price or better. Investors would use a limit order to establish a price at which they are willing to trade.

LIMIT PRICE – The price specified by an investor for a limit order. For an order to write options, this represents the lowest price the investor will accept.

LONG-TERM – Relates to the gain or loss in a security that has been held for a certain period of time. For example, to qualify as a long-term capital gain under current tax laws, a security must be held for twelve months or more.

MARGIN (ACCOUNT) – A feature of a brokerage account which permits an investor to borrow funds through the broker to purchase additional securities, thus providing investment leverage. The term also refers to the amount of equity in an account (securities or cash) a broker requires to support an uncovered option position.

MARGIN CALL – A call by the broker for additional funds or securities to be added to the margin account when the value of the equity in the account has declined below minimum requirements.

MARKET ORDER – An order for immediate execution at the best price available when the order reaches the exchange.

MOVING AVERAGE – A series of successive averages in a set of numbers. As a new number is added, the last number in the series is deleted.

NAKED – An option transaction that is opened whereby the investor does not own the underlying security (also called "uncovered"). An investor writing a naked put or call option on 100 shares of the QQQQ, for example, does not own the shares.

ODD LOT – Refers to fewer than 100 shares of a common stock or ETF.

OPEN INTEREST – The total number of option contracts for a stock or ETF option that are in existence at any given time.

OPTION – A contract permitting the holder (buyer) to purchase (call) or sell (put) a stock or ETF at a fixed price (strike) until a specific date (expiration).

OPTION AGREEMENT – A written document that must be signed by an option investor and given to the brokerage firm before the investor may be approved for trading in options. The purpose of the agreement is to help assure that the investor has adequate financial resources, trading experience and/or knowledge and that the investor's goals are appropriate for the type of option transactions the investor is asking the brokerage firm to provide. The investor is also supplied with a copy of *Characteristics and Risks of Standardized Options.*

OPTION CHAIN – A string of option quotes for a specific stock or ETF which includes every expiration date and strike price available for options on that security. This is typically provided by online brokers as a part of their automated quotation service to simplify the identification of ticker symbols for options and to facilitate obtaining quotes and executing trades.

OPTION CONTRACT – An agreement by an option writer to sell (call) or buy (put) a given security at a predetermined price (strike) until a certain date (expiration). The holder (buyer) of the option is not obligated to exercise (act on) the option, but the seller (writer) of the option must perform the obligation if the buyer exercises rights under the option contract.

OPTION CYCLE – Each stock and ETF is given a series of four months during which option contracts expire. Options for a stock or ETF generally expire on the same four months every year, plus the current month and the next following month.

OPTIONS CLEARING CORPORATION – Referred to as the OCC, it is an organization established in 1972 to process and guarantee options transactions that take place on the organized exchanges.

ORDINARY INCOME – Income from sources such as wages, dividends and interest. These items of income do not qualify for special tax treatment. Short-term capital gains are also taxed as ordinary income.

OUT-OF-THE-MONEY - The strike price of a put option is below the market price of the underlying shares or the strike price of a call option is above the market price. For example, the put option for a security with a strike price of $55 when the shares are trading at $58 would be $3 out-of-the-money.

PREMIUM – The current price at which an option contract trades and the amount a buyer would pay and a seller would receive. The amount of the premium is determined by a variety of factors, including the time remaining to expiration, the strike price chosen, the price and volatility of the underlying shares, and interest rates.

PUT – An option permitting the holder (buyer) to sell a stock or ETF at a predetermined price until a certain date. For example, an investor may purchase a put option on AAA shares giving the investor the right to sell 100 shares (for each option contract) at $50 per share until September 15.

PUT OPTION WRITING (UNCOVERED) – An investment strategy for investors who are generally seeking to increase income by selling (writing) puts on individual stocks or ETFs. The option writer receives premium income in exchange for assuring that the buyer of the option can sell the shares at the agreed price during the operative time period of the option contract.

RESISTANCE – Increased supply in the shares of a security, which may cause its price to top out at a certain level.

ROLLING DOWN – Buying back an option position and then writing a new option with the same expiration, but with a lower strike price.

ROLLING FORWARD – Buying back an option position and then writing a new option at the same strike price, but with a longer expiration.

ROLLING UP – Buying back an option position and then writing a new option with the same expiration, but with a higher strike price.

ROUND LOT – For common stocks and ETFs the standard unit of trading is a round lot, which is 100 shares or a multiple thereof.

SECURITIES & EXCHANGE COMMISSION (SEC) – The federal agency that administers securities laws in the United States. The SEC, created under the Securities Exchange Act of 1934, governs the following: registration of organized securities exchanges, proxy solicitation, disclosure requirements for securities in the secondary market and regulation of insider trading. This Act, along with the Securities Act of 1933, forms the basis of securities regulation.

SELL-TO-OPEN – The placing of an initial order by an option writer to sell an option in order to establish a position. The writer receives premium income from the buyer of the option.

SHORT POSITION – Regarding options, an investment position where the investor has written an option with the contract obligation remaining outstanding.

SHORT SALE – Regarding stocks or ETFs, the sale of securities that are not owned by the seller in anticipation of repurchasing at a lower price and profiting by the spread.

SHORT-TERM – Relates to the gain or loss in a security that has been held for a certain period of time. For example, under current tax laws the gain or loss in a security held for less than one year would be short-term.

STRIKE PRICE – The price at which the holder (buyer) of a put option can sell the underlying shares or the holder (buyer) of a call option can purchase the underlying shares. Also sometimes referred to as the "exercise price."

SUPPORT – Increased demand for the shares of a security, which may cause its price to bottom out at a certain level.

TECHNICAL ANALYSIS – An attempt to identify trends in supply and demand for a security through analysis of variables such as price levels, price movements and trading volume.

TECHNICAL INDICATORS – Chart formations used in technical analysis to determine the timing of investments and the selection of investments.

TICKER SYMBOL – The abbreviation for a stock, ETF or option used on securities quotation machines. For example, "FFF" is the ETF ticker symbol for the Fortune 500 Index Tracking ETF and "FFFTM" is the option ticker symbol for FFF puts with an August expiration and a strike price of $65.

TIME VALUE - That part of an option's market price which is solely attributable to the remaining time before the expiration of the option. If the option is out-of-the-money or at-the-money, the entire premium is attributable to time value. If the option is in-the-money, the amount attributable to time value is calculated by subtracting the amount by which the option is in-the-money from the current option premium. For example, if the current market price of an option is $3 ½ and the option is in-the-money by $2, the time value is $1 ½.

UNCOVERED (PUT or CALL) – An option transaction that is opened whereby the investor does not own the underlying security (also called "naked"). An investor writing an uncovered put or call option on 100 shares of the QQQQ, for example, does not own the shares.

UNDERLYING SECURITY/SHARES – The stock or ETF that, in the case of a put or call contract, the option holder (buyer) has the right, but not the obligation, to sell to the put writer or buy from the call writer according to the terms of the option contract.

UNREALIZED GAIN – Occurs when the value of an unsold asset rises above its original cost. Also referred to as a "paper gain."

UNREALIZED LOSS – Occurs when the value of an unsold asset is reduced below its original cost. Also referred to as a "paper loss."

APPENDIX

SUGGESTED READING

BOOKS ABOUT STOCKS

The Wall Street Journal Guide To Under-Standing Money & Investing by Kenneth M. Morris, Virginia B. Morris, Alan M. Siegel, paperback, 160 pages. This handy fact-filled book initiates you into the mysteries of the financial pages...buying stocks, bonds, mutual funds, futures and options, spotting trends and evaluating companies. A good beginning level investment book. Currently available over the Internet through Amazon.com.

Stocks for the Long Run – The Definitive Guide to Financial Market Returns and Long-Term Investment Strategies by Jeremy J. Siegel, Professor of Finance-the Wharton School of the University of Pennsylvania, hardcover, 388 pages. Siegel's book is a comprehensive and highly readable history of the stock market that dramatically makes the case for long-term investing in stocks. It is probably the best comprehensive text available about the market. An excellent reference for seasoned investors and anyone else interested in how the market works. Currently available over the Internet through Amazon.com.

BOOKS BY THIS AUTHOR ABOUT
WRITING COVERED CALLS AND PUT WRITING

Covered Call Writing Demystified: Double-Digit Returns on Stocks in a Slower Growth Market for the Conservative Investor by Paul D. Kadavy, comb bound, 328 pages. The definitive education and guide for enhancing the investment returns on your stocks through covered call writing. Includes calculation software using Excel®. Currently available through www.arrowpublications.net at a discount.

Covered Call Writing With Exchange Traded Funds (ETFs): Double-Digit Returns, Diversification, Downside Protection by Paul D. Kadavy, comb bound, 182 pages. A complete program for enhancing your investment returns by utilizing covered call writing specifically for Exchange Traded Funds, the hottest new equity investments available today that are increasingly replacing mutual funds. Lists all current ETFs, which offer call writing and a ranking for attractiveness. Includes calculation software using Excel®. Currently available through www.arrowpublications.net at a discount.

Covered Call Writing With Qs & Diamonds: Double-Digit Returns on Ready-Made Portfolios by Paul D. Kadavy, comb bound, 174 pages. The covered call writing program specifically geared to two of the most popular and highly liquid ETFs that offer strike prices for call writing in $1 increments. Includes calculation software using Excel®. Currently available through www.arrowpublications.net at a discount.

Put Option Writing Demystified: Earn Double-Digit Cash Returns While Waiting to Buy Stocks at a Discount by Paul D. Kadavy, 176 pages. The only book devoted exclusively to the subject of a little-known, often misunderstood investment opportunity known as "put option writing." Includes calculation software using Excel®. Currently available through www.arrowpublications.net at a discount.

Short Spider Straddles: A Winning Combination by Paul D. Kadavy, 77 pages. A ready-to-implement-yourself program designed to achieve long-term double-digit compounded returns. The program requires no knowledge of stocks, no investment research, no big investment, and is incredibly easy to implement, requiring only about 15 minutes per month. Includes calculation software using Excel® and historical back testing data. Currently available through www.arrowpublications.net at a discount.

A SAMPLING OF EXCHANGE TRADED FUNDS

ETF NAME	SYMBOL	CATEGORY	OPTIONS OFFERED?
BLDRS Asia 50 ADR Index Fund	ADRA	INTERNATIONAL	NO
BLDRS Developed markets 100 ADR Index Fund	ADRD	INTERNATIONAL	NO
BLDRS Emerging markets 50 ADR Index Fund	ADRE	INTERNATIONAL	NO
BLDRS Europe 100 ADR Index Fund	ADRU	INTERNATIONAL	NO
iShares Lehman Aggregate Bond Fund	AGG	BOND	YES
Merrill Lynch Biotech HOLDRS	BBH	SECTOR	YES
Merrill Lynch Broadband HOLDRS	BDH	SECTOR	YES
Merrill Lynch B2B Internet HOLDRS	BHH	SECTOR	YES
streetTRACKS D.J. Global Titans Index Fund	DGT	BROAD BASED	YES
DIAMONDS Trust Series I	DIA	BROAD BASED	YES
streetTRACKS D.J. U.S. Small Cap Growth Index Fund	DSG	BROAD BASED	NO
streetTRACKS D.J. U.S. Small Cap Value Index Fund	DSV	BROAD BASED	NO
iShares D. J. Select Dividend Index Fund	DVY	BROAD BASED	YES
iShares MSCI Emerging Index Fund	EEM	INTERNATIONAL	NO
iShares MSCI - EAFE	EFA	INTERNATIONAL	YES
Merrill Lynch Europe 2001 HOLDRS	EKH	INTERNATIONAL	YES
streetTRACKS D.J. U.S. Large Cap Growth Index Fund	ELG	BROAD BASED	NO
streetTRACKS D.J. U.S. Large Cap Value Index Fund	ELV	BROAD BASED	NO
iShares MSCI Pacific Ex-Japan Index Fund	EPP	INTERNATIONAL	NO
iShares MSCI - Australia	EWA	INTERNATIONAL	NO
iShares MSCI - Canada	EWC	INTERNATIONAL	NO
iShares MSCI - Sweden	EWD	INTERNATIONAL	NO
iShares MSCI - Germany	EWG	INTERNATIONAL	NO
iShares MSCI - Hong Kong	EWH	INTERNATIONAL	NO
iShares MSCI - Italy	EWI	INTERNATIONAL	NO
iShares MSCI - Japan	EWJ	INTERNATIONAL	NO
iShares MSCI - Belgium	EWK	INTERNATIONAL	NO
iShares MSCI - Switzerland	EWL	INTERNATIONAL	NO
iShares MSCI - Malaysia (Free)	EWM	INTERNATIONAL	NO
iShares MSCI - Netherlands	EWN	INTERNATIONAL	NO
iShares MSCI - Austria	EWO	INTERNATIONAL	NO
iShares MSCI - Spain	EWP	INTERNATIONAL	NO
iShares MSCI - France	EWQ	INTERNATIONAL	NO
iShares MSCI - Singapore (Free)	EWS	INTERNATIONAL	NO
iShares MSCI - Taiwan	EWT	INTERNATIONAL	NO
iShares MSCI - United Kingdom	EWU	INTERNATIONAL	NO
iShares MSCI - Mexico (Free)	EWW	INTERNATIONAL	NO
iShares MSCI - South Korea	EWY	INTERNATIONAL	NO
iShares MSCI - Brazil	EWZ	INTERNATIONAL	NO

WRITING UNCOVERED PUT AND CALL COMBINATIONS

iShares MSCI South Africa Index Fund	EZA	INTERNATIONAL	NO
iShares MSCI - European Monitary Union Index Fund	EZU	INTERNATIONAL	NO
streetTRACKS Dow Jones STOXX 50 Fund	FEU	INTERNATIONAL	NO
streetTRACKS Dow Jones EURO STOXX 50 Fund	FEZ	INTERNATIONAL	NO
iShares FTSE/Xinhua China 25 Index Fund	FXI	INTERNATIONAL	YES
streetTRACKS Gold Shares	GLD	SECTOR	NO
Merrill Lynch Internet HOLDRS	HHH	SECTOR	YES
Merrill Lynch Internet Architecture HOLDRS	IAH	SECTOR	YES
Vanguard Telecommunication Services VIPERs	IAU	SECTOR	NO
iShares NASDAQ Biotechnology Index Fund	IBB	SECTOR	YES
iShares Cohen & Steers Realty Majors Index Fund	ICF	SECTOR	YES
iShares D.J. U.S. Utilities Sector Index Fund	IDU	SECTOR	YES
iShares Lehman 7-10 Year Treasury Bond Fund	IEF	BOND	YES
iShares S&P Europe 350	IEV	INTERNATIONAL	NO
iShares Goldman Sachs Natural Resources Index Fund	IGE	SECTOR	NO
iShares Goldman Sachs Technology Index Fund	IGM	SECTOR	YES
iShares Goldman Sachs Network Index Fund	IGN	SECTOR	YES
iShares Goldman Sachs Software Index Fund	IGV	SECTOR	YES
iShares Goldman Sachs Semiconductor Index Fund	IGW	SECTOR	YES
Merrill Lynch Internet Infrastructure HOLDRS	IIH	SECTOR	YES
iShares S&P MidCap 400 Index Fund	IJH	BROAD BASED	YES
iShares S&P MidCap 400/BARRA Value	IJJ	BROAD BASED	YES
iShares S&P MidCap 400/BARRA Growth	IJK	BROAD BASED	YES
iShares S&P SmallCap 600 Index Fund	IJR	BROAD BASED	YES
iShares Small Cap 600/BARRA Value Index Fund	IJS	BROAD BASED	YES
iShares Small Cap 600/BARRA Growth Index Fund	IJT	BROAD BASED	YES
iShares S&P Latin America 40 Index Fund	ILF	INTERNATIONAL	NO
iShares S&P Global 100 Index Fund	IOO	INTERNATIONAL	NO
iShares S&P 1500 Index Fund	ISI	BROAD BASED	NO
iShares S&P TOPIX 150 Index Fund	ITF	INTERNATIONAL	NO
iShares S&P 500/BARRA Value Index Fund	IVE	BROAD BASED	NO
iShares S&P 500 Index Fund	IVV	BROAD BASED	NO
iShares S&P 500/BARRA Growth Index Fund	IVW	BROAD BASED	NO
iShares Russell 1000 Index Fund	IWB	BROAD BASED	YES
iShares Trust Russell Microcap	IWC	BROAD BASED	YES
iShares Russell 1000 Value Index Fund	IWD	BROAD BASED	YES
iShares Russell 1000 Growth Index Fund	IWF	BROAD BASED	YES
iShares Russell 2000 Index Fund	IWM	BROAD BASED	YES
iShares Russell 2000 Value Index Fund	IWN	BROAD BASED	YES
iShares Russell 2000 Growth Index Fund	IWO	BROAD BASED	YES
iShares Russell MidCap Growth Index Fund	IWP	BROAD BASED	YES
iShares Russell MidCap Index Fund	IWR	BROAD BASED	YES
iShares Russell MidCap Value Index Fund	IWS	BROAD BASED	YES
iShares Russell 3000 Index Fund	IWV	BROAD BASED	YES
iShares Russell 3000 Value Index Fund	IWW	BROAD BASED	YES
iShares Russell 3000 Growth Index Fund	IWZ	BROAD BASED	YES
iShares S&P Global Energy Index Fund	IXC	SECTOR	NO
iShares S&P Global Financial Index Fund	IXG	SECTOR	NO
iShares S&P Global Healthcare Index Fund	IXJ	SECTOR	NO
iShares S&P Global Info Technology Index Fund	IXN	SECTOR	NO
iShares S&P Global Telecommunications Index Fund	IXP	SECTOR	NO
iShares D.J. U.S. Consumer Cyclical Sector Index Fund	IYC	SECTOR	NO

WRITING UNCOVERED PUT AND CALL COMBINATIONS

iShares D.J. U.S. Energy Sector Index Fund	IYE	SECTOR	YES
iShares D.J. U.S. Financial Sector Index Fund	IYF	SECTOR	YES
iShares D.J. U.S. Financial Services Sector Index Fund	IYG	SECTOR	NO
iShares D.J. U.S. Healthcare Sector Index Fund	IYH	SECTOR	YES
iShares D.J. U.S. Industrial Sector Index Fund	IYJ	SECTOR	NO
iShares D.J. U.S. Cons. Non-Cyclical Sector Index Fund	IYK	SECTOR	NO
iShares D.J. U.S. Basic Materials Sector Index Fund	IYM	SECTOR	NO
iShares D.J. U.S. Real Estate Index Fund	IYR	SECTOR	YES
iShares D.J. Transportation Average Index Fund	IYT	SECTOR	NO
iShares D.J. U.S. Technology Sector Index Fund	IYW	SECTOR	YES
iShares D.J. U.S. Total Market Index Fund	IYY	BROAD BASED	YES
iShares D.J. U.S. Telecom. Sector Index Fund	IYZ	SECTOR	YES
iShares Morningstar Large Core Index Fund	JKD	BROAD BASED	NO
iShares Morningstar Large Growth Index Fund	JKE	BROAD BASED	NO
iShares Morningstar Large Value Index Fund	JKF	BROAD BASED	NO
iShares Morningstar Mid Core Index Fund	JKG	BROAD BASED	NO
iShares Morningstar Mid Core Index Fund	JKH	BROAD BASED	NO
iShares Morningstar Mid Value Index Fund	JKI	BROAD BASED	NO
iShares Morningstar Small Core Index Fund	JKJ	BROAD BASED	NO
iShares Morningstar Small Growth Index Fund	JKK	BROAD BASED	NO
iShares Morningstar Small Value Index Fund	JKL	BROAD BASED	NO
iShares GS $ InvesTopTM Corporate Bond Fund	LQD	BOND	YES
MidCap SPDR Trust Series I	MDY	BROAD BASED	YES
Merrill Lynch Market 2000+ HOLDRS	MKH	BROAD BASED	YES
streetTRACKS Morgan Stanley Technology Index Fund	MTK	SECTOR	NO
iShares NYSE 100 Index Fund	NY	BROAD BASED	YES
iShares NYSE Composite Index Fund	NYC	BROAD BASED	YES
iShares S&P 100 Index Fund	OEF	BROAD BASED	YES
Merrill Lynch Market Oil Service HOLDRS	OIH	SECTOR	YES
Fidelity NASDAQ Composite Index Tracking Stock	ONEQ	BROAD BASED	YES
SPDR O-Strip Exchange Traded Fund	OOO	BROAD BASED	YES
PowerShares High Yield Equity Dividend Achievers	PEY	BROAD BASED	YES
PowerShares Golden Dragon Halter USX China	PGJ	INTERNATIONAL	YES
Merrill Lynch Pharmaceutical HOLDRS	PPH	SECTOR	YES
PowerShares Dynamic Market Portfolio	PWC	BROAD BASED	YES
PowerShares Dynamic OTC Portfolio	PWO	BROAD BASED	YES
PowerShares QQQ	QQQQ	BROAD BASED	YES
Merrill Lynch Regional Bank HOLDRS	RKH	SECTOR	YES
Rydex ETF Trust	RSP	BROAD BASED	NO
Merrill Lynch Retail HOLDRS	RTH	SECTOR	YES
streetTRACKS Wilshire REIT Index Fund	RWR	SECTOR	NO
iShares Lehman 1-3 Year Treasury Bond Fund	SHY	BOND	YES
Merrill Lynch Semiconductor HOLDRS	SMH	SECTOR	YES
SPDR Trust Series I	SPY	BROAD BASED	YES
Merrill Lynch Software HOLDRS	SWH	SECTOR	YES
iShares Lehman TIPS Bond Fund	TIP	BOND	YES
iShares Lehman 20 Year Treasury Bond Fund	TLT	BOND	YES
Merrill Lynch Telecom HOLDRS	TTH	SECTOR	YES
Merrill Lynch Utilities HOLDRS	UTH	SECTOR	YES
Fortune 500 Index Tracking Stock	TMW	BROAD BASED	YES
Vanguard Materials Index Fund; VIPERs	VAW	SECTOR	NO

Vanguard Small-Cap Index Fund; VIPERs	VB	BROAD BASED	NO
Vanguard Small-Cap Growth VIPERs	VBK	BROAD BASED	YES
Vanguard Small-Cap Value Index Fund; VIPERs	VBR	BROAD BASED	NO
Vanguard Consumer Discretionary Index Fund; VIPERs	VCR	SECTOR	NO
Vanguard Consumer Staples Index Fund; VIPERs	VDC	SECTOR	NO
Vanguard Energy Index Fund; VIPERs	VDE	SECTOR	NO
Vanguard Financials Index Fund; VIPERs	VFH	SECTOR	NO
Vanguard European VIPERs	VGK	INTERNATIONAL	NO
Vanguard Information Technology Index Fund; VIPERs	VGT	SECTOR	NO
Vanguard Healthcare Index Fund; VIPERs	VHT	SECTOR	NO
Vanguard Industrials Index Fund; VIPERs	VIS	SECTOR	NO
Vanguard REIT Index Fund; VIPERs	VNQ	SECTOR	NO
Vanguard Mid-Cap Index Fund; VIPERs	VO	BROAD BASED	NO
Vanguard Telecomm. Services Index Fund; VIPERs	VOX	SECTOR	NO
Vanguard Pacific VIPERs	VPL	INTERNATIONAL	YES
Vanguard Utilities Index Fund; VIPERs	VPU	SECTOR	NO
Vanguard Total Stock Market; VIPERs	VTI	BROAD BASED	YES
Vanguard Value Index Fund; VIPERs	VTV	BROAD BASED	NO
Vanguard Growth Index Fund; VIPERs	VUG	BROAD BASED	NO
Vanguard Large-Cap Index Fund; VIPERs	VV	BROAD BASED	NO
Vanguard Emerging Markets VIPERs	VWO	BROAD BASED	NO
Vanguard Extended Market; VIPERs	VXF	BROAD BASED	NO
Merrill Lynch Wireless HOLDRS	WMH	SECTOR	YES
Select Sector SPDR Fund - Basic Industries	XLB	SECTOR	YES
Select Sector SPDR Fund - Energy Select Sector	XLE	SECTOR	YES
Select Sector SPDR Fund - Financial	XLF	SECTOR	YES
Select Sector SPDR Fund - Industrial	XLI	SECTOR	YES
Select Sector SPDR Fund - Technology	XLK	SECTOR	YES
Select Sector SPDR Fund - Consumer Staples	XLP	SECTOR	YES
Select Sector SPDR Fund - Utilities	XLU	SECTOR	YES
Select Sector SPDR Fund - Consumer Services	XLV	SECTOR	YES
Select Sector SPDR Fund - Cyclical/Transportation	XLY	SECTOR	YES

Note: D.J. = Dow Jones

OPTION, BROKERAGE & ETF WEB SITES ON THE INTERNET

The following Web sites may be useful to those desiring information about options, discount brokers, charts, technical analysis and ETFs.

OPTIONS

www.cboe.com – Chicago Board Options Exchange. This is the largest exchange for trading options. The CBOE Web site is a tremendously valuable resource about how options work. This is probably the best educational site about options available to the nonprofessional. The booklet *Characteristics and Risks of Standardized Options* is available on this Web site. Delayed quotes on ETFs and ETF option chains are also available.

www.888options.com – The Options Industry Council. The OIC is a non-profit organization created to educate the investing public and brokers about the benefits and risks of exchange-traded options. In addition to providing a great deal of options related education on this site, the OIC also conducts free seminars around the country. The schedule for these seminars is provided on the site.

DISCOUNT BROKERAGES

All of the following provide quotes on various securities and online investment capabilities for options, Exchange Traded Funds (including the QQQQ and the DIA), bonds, mutual funds, and other types of investments. Some provide general business news, company specific news, investment research, charts (many including sophisticated technical analysis) and other information. This list is not meant to be exhaustive, but is representative of the largest online discount brokers. Information on these and other companies is available at libraries for non-computer users.

www.fidelity.com - Fidelity Investments; 800-544-5555

www.schwab.com - Charles Schwab & Co.; 800-2-schwab

www.tdameritrade.com - TD Ameritrade; 800-454-9272

www.etrade.com - E-Trade; 800-etrade1

www.scottrade.com – Scottrade; 800-619-save

CHARTS AND TECHNICAL ANALYSIS

www.bigcharts.com – BigCharts.com

www.stockcharts.com – StockCharts.com

Note: All online broker sites offer varying degrees of charting and technical analysis to their customers.

EXCHANGE TRADED FUNDS

www.bloomberg.com – Web site of Bloomberg.com. For information about ETFs click on "ETFs."

www.nasdaq.com – Web site of the NASDAQ stock market. For information about ETFs click on "ETFs."

INDEX

ABOUT THE AUTHOR

As a thirty-year career banker and trust officer for Norwest Corporation, now Wells Fargo & Co., one of the nation's largest financial institutions, Paul D. Kadavy was president of numerous banks in three states. He also headed a multi-billion dollar trust department, managed a team of investment professionals, and was a trusted advisor to many of the banks' individual clients. He also subsequently served as president and chief executive officer for another banking enterprise in Las Vegas, Nevada. Now retired from banking, he is a writer, teacher and public speaker.

Kadavy has served as a faculty member of the National Graduate Trust School at Northwestern University, The Schools of Banking, Inc., the American Institute of Banking and numerous community colleges in several states. He was a lecturer on trust, investment and banking subjects to FDIC and Federal Reserve Bank examiners in Washington, D.C. He has been a public speaker for the past twenty-five years.

In addition to authoring *Writing Uncovered Put and Call Combinations*, Kadavy has also written the novel *Scattered Ashes* and financial books including *Covered Call Writing Demystified*, *Covered Call Writing with Exchange Traded Funds (ETFs)*, *Covered Call Writing with Qs and Diamonds*, *Put Option Writing Demystified*, *Short Spider Straddles*, *Put and Call Option Writing for the Investment Advisor and Financial Planner*, *Personal Cash Flow and Net Worth Planning Demystified* and *The Book of World-Class Quotations: The Best of the Best Quotations on Earth*.

His books are available on the Internet through Arrow Publications (www.arrowpublications.net and www.advisor-options.com) and Amazon.com.

He is the author of banking, trust and investment articles for such national publications as *Financial Review*, *Trusts & Estates*, *Pension World*, *The Collector/Investor*, *Cases & Comment* and *American Bankers Association Trust Management*.